# SpringerBriefs in Regional Science

**Series Editors**

Henk Folmer, University of Groningen, Groningen, The Netherlands

Mark Partridge, Ohio State University, Columbus, USA

Daniel P. McMillen, University of Illinois, Urbana, USA

Andrés Rodríguez-Pose, London School of Economics, London, UK

Henry W. C. Yeung, National University of Singapore, Singapore, Singapore

T0349483

SpringerBriefs present concise summaries of cutting-edge research and practical applications across a wide spectrum of fields. Featuring compact, authored volumes of 50 to 125 pages, the series covers a range of content from professional to academic. SpringerBriefs in Regional Science showcase emerging theory, empirical research and practical application, lecture notes and reviews in spatial and regional science from a global author community.

All titles in this book series are peer-reviewed. This series is indexed in SCOPUS.

Tomasz Kijek • Arkadiusz Kijek •
Anna Matras-Bolibok

# Innovation and Regional Technological Convergence

Theory and Evidence

 Springer

Tomasz Kijek [iD]
Department of Microeconomics
and Applied Economics
Maria Curie-Skłodowska University
Lublin, Poland

Arkadiusz Kijek [iD]
Department of Statistics and Econometrics
Maria Curie-Skłodowska University
Lublin, Poland

Anna Matras-Bolibok [iD]
Department of Microeconomics
and Applied Economics
Maria Curie-Skłodowska University
Lublin, Poland

This work was supported by National Science Centre, Poland (2017/27/B/HS4/00893)

ISSN 2192-0427          ISSN 2192-0435   (electronic)
SpringerBriefs in Regional Science
ISBN 978-3-031-24530-5        ISBN 978-3-031-24531-2   (eBook)
https://doi.org/10.1007/978-3-031-24531-2

This Springer imprint is published by the registered company Springer Nature Switzerland AG
The registered company address is: Gewerbestrasse 11, 6330 Cham, Switzerland

# Acknowledgments

The authors thank Hugo Hollanders from UNU-MERIT, Maastricht University for providing access to the latest and historical datasets of the Regional Innovation Scoreboard.

This book comes out as a part of the research project financed by the National Science Centre, Poland on the basis of decision number 2017/27/B/HS4/00893.

# Contents

# Chapter 1
# Introduction

The concept of income convergence has drawn the attention of many economists involved in the growth debate (Alataş, 2021). Recent theories of growth and empirical studies suggest that heterogeneity with respect to technological conditions in general and total factor productivity—TFP in particular are identified as the most decisive factors for the rate of income convergence of countries (Islam, 2003). Apparently, depending on whether initial TFP differences decrease or increase over time, income convergence or divergence may be a matter of fact. This has directed researchers' attention to the concept of technological (TFP) convergence.

Although many empirical studies try to find the answer to the question of technological convergence at the country level (Dowrick & Nguyen, 1989; Wolf, 1991; Dougherty & Jorgenson, 1997; Tebaldi, 2016; Rath & Akram, 2019), regional technological convergence is the research area of relatively modest exploration. However, this situation started to change, since the importance of technological convergence and its determinants have progressively gained attention in both the scientific and the policy domains at the regional level (Rodil-Marzábal & Vence-Deza, 2020). In the context of the Lisbon Agenda (European Council, 2000) and the Europe 2020 strategy (Commission of the European Communities, 2010) goals of making Europe and its regions the most competitive and dynamic knowledge-based economies in the world, it seems crucial to find whether innovation, regarded as the main driver of regional TFP growth (Dettori et al., 2012), can stimulate technological convergence and under what conditions.

Empirical findings suggest that innovation can lead to both technological convergence and divergence processes across regional economies (Walker & Storper, 1989; Verspagen, 2010). In the former, thanks to the diffusion of knowledge and innovation, it is possible for the regions which are technologically lagging behind to catch up with the regions with a higher level of technological advancement. On the other hand, innovations provide additional technological rent and allow leaders to speed up in the technology race. Due to the specificity of knowledge, including its cumulative nature, the relations between the catching-up and speeding-up processes

© The Author(s) 2023
T. Kijek et al., *Innovation and Regional Technological Convergence*, SpringerBriefs in Regional Science, https://doi.org/10.1007/978-3-031-24531-2_1

depend on the initial innovative potential of the regions and their absorptive capacities (Dosi, 1988; Verspagen, 2010; Roper & Love, 2006).

From the theoretical perspective, TFP catching-up process can be explained by the concept of 'advantage of backwardness' (Vu & Asongu, 2019) and the semi-endogenous R&D-based growth models and their extensions to the regional framework (Jones, 1995; Kortum, 1997; Fukuda, 2017). On the other hand, the conclusion drawn from the first generation of R&D-based endogenous growth models (Segerstrom et al., 1990; Grossman & Helpman, 1991; Baldwin et al., 2001) suggest that a TFP gap between technological leaders and technological followers may widen by R&D investments. Interestingly, the multiple equilibria Schumpeterian R&D models (Howitt & Mayer-Foulkes, 2005) permit the conclusion that different strategies for technology creation and adoption induce convergence clubs formation in TFP. Regional heterogeneity of technology level and the existence of convergence clubs may be also explained by local technological or knowledge spillovers and regional innovation and technological policies, which become more similar over time within certain groups.

The possible multimodality of the distribution of TFP may be also anchored in the theory of innovation geography (Feldman & Kogler, 2010). In the spatial context, the local growth depends on the amount of innovation activity which is carried out locally, and possibly on the ability to take advantage of external technological achievements. At the regional level, technology spillovers have an important spatial component, as it has been argued that spillovers do not travel easily, so that the performance of an individual region is influenced by its geographical location. The existence of localized spillovers of technological knowledge plays a significant role in the regional technological convergence process as the propensity to innovate of each region does depend on that of the surrounding areas. Allowing unequal distribution of TFP, special attention should be paid to the localized spreading of innovation activities.

In the light of the presented considerations, the main aim of this book is to explore the role of innovation in technological convergence in the European regional area. The theoretical framework of the analyses is presented in Chaps. 2 and 3. The former focuses on the spatial aspects of innovation activities, knowledge-based foundation of regional development and policy framework of innovation-driven growth of EU regions. The latter presents the concept of convergence with special reference to technological convergence. Importantly, it gives insights into the role of innovation in technological convergence from the point of view of alternative R&D-based growth theories. In turn, Chap. 4 contains the methodology of research and the results of analyses. We test stochastic convergence, absolute and conditional β-convergence, as well as club convergence. In our analyses we consider technology and innovation spillovers and their impact on the rate of technological convergence. Such approach to testing technological convergence in the European regional area enables us possible to capture a comprehensive picture of the role of innovation activities in shaping TFP trajectories.

We believe that our book will be appealing to researchers interested in regional development, economic and spatial aspects of science and technology progress, and economics of innovation and knowledge. Practitioners and policy-makers may also find it useful as a source of recent results in economic cohesion and technological convergence.

# References

Alataş, S. (2021). Revisiting the Solow growth model: New empirical evidence on the convergence debate. *Journal of Economic and Administrative Sciences.* https://doi.org/10.1108/JEAS-02-2021-0035

Baldwin, R. E., Martin, P., & Ottaviano, G. I. (2001). Global income divergence, trade and industrialisation: The geography of growth take-offs. *Journal of Economic Growth, 6*(1), 5–37.

Commission of the European Communities. (2010). *Europe 2020. A strategy for smart, suitable and inclusive growth.* COM (2010)2020. European Commission.

Dettori, B., Marrocu, E., & Paci, R. (2012). Total factor productivity, intangible assets and spatial dependence in the European regions. *Regional Studies, 46*(10), 1401–1416. https://doi.org/10.1080/00343404.2010.529288

Dosi, G. (1988). Sources, procedures, and microeconomic effects of innovation. *Journal of Economic Literature, 26*(3), 1120–1171.

Dougherty, C., & Jorgenson, D. W. (1997). There is no silver bullet: Investment and growth in the G7. *National Institute Economic Review, 162*(1), 57–74. https://doi.org/10.1177/002795019716200105

Dowrick, S., & Nguyen, D. (1989). OECD comparative economic growth 1950–85: Catch-up and convergence. *American Economic Review, 79*(5), 1010–1030.

European Council. (2000). *Presidency conclusions Lisbon European council. 23–24 March 2000 (no. 100/1/00).* European Council.

Feldman, M. P., & Kogler, D. F. (2010). Stylized facts in the geography of innovation. In R. Hall & N. Rosenberg (Eds.), *Handbook of the economics of innovation* (Vol. 1, pp. 381–410). Elsevier. https://doi.org/10.1016/s0169-7218(10)01008-7

Fukuda, K. (2017). The effects of globalization on regional inequality in a model of semi-endogenous growth and footloose capital. *Asia-Pacific Journal of Accounting & Economics, 24*(1–2), 95–105. https://doi.org/10.1080/16081625.2015.1062243

Grossman, G. M., & Helpman, E. (1991). *Innovation and growth in the global economy.* MIT Press.

Howitt, P., & Mayer-Foulkes, D. (2005). R/D, implementation, and stagnation: A Schumpeterian theory of convergence clubs. *Journal of Money, Credit, and Banking, 37*(1), 147–177. https://doi.org/10.1353/mcb.2005.0006

Islam, N. (2003). Productivity dynamics in a large sample of countries: A panel study. *Review of Income and Wealth, 49*(2), 247–272.

Jones, C. (1995). R&D-based models of economic growth. *Journal of Political Economy, 103*(4), 759–784.

Kortum, S. (1997). Research, patenting, and technological change. *Econometrica, 65*(6), 1389–1419. https://doi.org/10.2307/2171741

Rath, B. N., & Akram, V. (2019). A reassessment of total factor productivity convergence: Evidence from cross-country analysis. *Economic Modelling, 82*, 87–98. https://doi.org/10.1016/j.econmod.2019.08.002

Rodil-Marzábal, Ó., & Vence-Deza, X. (2020). Regional innovation systems and regional disparities in the Euro area: Insights for regional innovation policy. In M. González-López & B. Asheim (Eds.), *Regions and innovation policies in Europe* (pp. 139–161). Edward Elgar. https://doi.org/10.4337/9781789904161.00012

Roper, S., & Love, J. H. (2006). Innovation and regional absorptive capacity: The labour market dimension. *The Annals of Regional Science, 40*(2), 437–447. https://doi.org/10.1007/s00168-006-0068-4

Segerstrom, P. S., Anant, T. C. A., & Dinopoulos, E. (1990). A Schumpeterian model of the product life cycle. *American Economic Review, 80*(5), 1077–1091.

Tebaldi, E. (2016). The dynamics of total factor productivity and institutions. *Journal of Economic Development, 41*(4), 1–25.

Verspagen, B. (2010). The spatial hierarchy of technological change and economic development in Europe. *The Annals of Regional Science, 45*(1), 109–132. https://doi.org/10.1007/s00168-009-0293-8

Vu, K. M., & Asongu, S. (2019). Backwardness advantage and economic growth in the information age: A cross-country empirical study. *Technological Forecasting and Social Change, 159*, 120197. https://doi.org/10.1016/j.techfore.2020.120197

Walker, R., & Storper, M. (1989). *The capitalist imperative: Territory, technology and industrial growth.* Basil Blackwell.

Wolf, E. N. (1991). Capital formation and productivity convergence over the long-term. *American Economic Review, 81*(3), 565–579.

# Chapter 2
# Innovation and Regional Development

## 2.1 Spatial Aspects of Innovation

Innovation is considered to be highly localized process. It does not appear in space uniformly, but is predominantly spatially concentrated (Crevoisier, 2004). A number of diverse theoretical and empirical frameworks have been developed to analyze spatial dimension of innovation. The theoretical approach to the relationship between innovation and local spaces was initially demonstrated in the concepts of 'new industrial districts' and 'innovative milieu'. The first of them, inspired by the Marshall's industrial district, was introduced by Becattini (Sforzi, 2015) to emphasize the dynamic linkages between the socio-cultural features of a productive community and the rate of growth of both its productivity and innovativeness (Becattini, 2002). Many theoretical considerations and empirical contributions reveal the impact of belonging to industrial districts on innovation performance (Boix et al., 2018; Boix-Domenech et al., 2019; Cainelli, 2008; Cainelli & De Liso, 2005; Muscio, 2006; Parra-Requena et al., 2020). The existence of dynamic efficiency in industrial districts in the form of positive innovation differentials with regard to the economy average, assigned to the existence of Marshallian external economies (economies of localization) is described by Boix and Galletto (2009) as an 'I-district effect'.

The second—'innovative milieu' approach, is considered to be a dynamic counterpart of the 'industrial district' concept, developed in the framework of the endogenous growth theory, providing more dynamic spatial elements related to synergies and collective learning, which explain innovation processes at the spatial level (Capello, 1998). In this concept, economic space is defined as a 'relational space' of cooperation, interpersonal synergies, and social collective actions that determine the innovation and economic performance of a given area (Camagni & Capello, 2002). The nature of these relationships should be both competitive and cooperative so that enterprises could act together in the common interest. The networks of synergy-producing interrelationships foster processes of cooperative

© The Author(s) 2023
T. Kijek et al., *Innovation and Regional Technological Convergence*, SpringerBriefs in Regional Science, https://doi.org/10.1007/978-3-031-24531-2_2

learning that help to reduce the uncertainty during technological breakthroughs and induce innovation locally (Simmie, 2005).

Spatial dimension of innovation is also presented in the learning region concept (Florida, 1995; Morgan, 2007). In line with this approach learning regions, as their name implies, are a central space for knowledge creation and provide an infrastructure which can facilitate the flows of knowledge, ideas, and learning (Florida, 1995). Boekema et al. (2000) suggest that distinction between the learning region (institutional networks that develop and implement a regional innovation strategy) and regional learning (mainly company-initiated cooperation between actors in a region through which they learn) should be considered. Learning through networking and interacting is seen as the main force that encourages firms to cluster in a given space and as the essential determinant of success of an innovative cluster (Breschi & Malerba, 2005). A substantial body of empirical research has convincingly shown that innovative activities tend to be spatially clustered. Audretsch and Feldman (1996) reveal that innovation has a strong tendency to cluster locally in regions where knowledge inputs are available and that the differences in spatial clustering depend on the stage of the industry life cycle and the importance of tacit knowledge. Also in Porter's (1990) 'competitive diamond' concept, the interactions between four sets of factors are more effective when the firms are clustered in space. The level of innovativeness of companies in a cluster is higher as they can take advantage of agglomeration economies, observe the competitors directly, benefit from collective knowledge and network-based effects as well as strengthened social interactions (Bell, 2005). Hassink (2005) proposed the concept of the learning cluster, that is able to bridge the gap between regional learning, that combines the strengths of both the learning region and clusters concept in tackling the problem of 'lock-ins' in regional economies.

The other paradigm in which space and innovation co-evolve is constituted by Regional Innovation System (RIS), a counterpart of National Innovation System (NIS) at the regional level (Cooke, 2008). In this concept, innovation is seen as dynamic and interactive learning process between companies and other organizations whose activities lead to initiation, diffusion, modification of new technologies, and determine the innovative performance of national firms (Freeman, 1995). In the triple-helix model, innovation is considered as the outcome of the interaction of three main groups of local actors: firms, government, and research institutions (Leydesdorff & Etzkowitz, 1998), whereas the quadruple-helix model, regarded as an enhancement of the triple-helix perspective, also includes a fourth component of the users and civil society (Höglund & Linton, 2018; Leydesdorff, 2012).

Spatial proximity and relatedness of the actors of innovation process matter for its effectiveness due to knowledge externalities appearance. Griliches (1992) defines knowledge spillovers as 'working on similar things and hence benefiting much from each other's research'. Knowledge externalities occur when the knowledge flows are not fully compensated and in situations where the protection of proprietary knowledge is incomplete (Karlsson & Gråsjö, 2014). That limited appropriability is considered to have, on the one hand, negative consequences in terms of missing incentives for entrepreneurs to generate knowledge, but on the other hand, also positive ones in terms of reduced knowledge costs (Antonelli & Colombelli, 2017). It could be thus stated that local knowledge may have the character of a (semi) public good, with properties of non-rivalry. It means that its use by one economic agent does not preclude the use by another economic actor (Roper et al., 2017). The empirical results indicate that knowledge externalities across space impact innovation performance (Bottazzi & Peri, 2003). Roper et al. (2013) reveal that knowledge externalities of openness are positively associated with firms' innovation performance by either increasing knowledge diffusion or strengthening competition. According to them, such externalities arise not simply from the (semi) public good nature of local knowledge but from the open innovation process itself. Positive social externalities resulting from openness in innovation may extend the sum of the achieved private benefits (Roper et al., 2013).

Co-location enables to establish contacts with potential cooperation partners and to exchange knowledge easier. A fundamental aspect of geographical proximity is the face-to-face contact between actors of innovation process, as it contributes to effective exchange of ideas and to spreading of knowledge as an externality. Face-to-face interactions have four main features: they are an efficient communication technology, they can help solve incentive problems, they can facilitate socialization and learning, and they provide psychological motivation (Storper & Venables, 2004).

The spatial dimension of innovation processes matters particularly for the flows of tacit knowledge. This type of knowledge is highly contextual and difficult to codify, and therefore is more easily transmitted through face-to-face contacts and personal relationships due to geographical proximity (Breschi & Lissoni, 2001). This type of knowledge is the cumulative output of long periods of learning, specific to a particular setting, and cannot easily be written down (Karlsson & Gråsjö, 2014). As Audretsch (1998) points out, the propensity for innovative activity to cluster spatially is highest in industries where tacit knowledge plays an important role. Successful innovation processes involve a mix of contextual and codified knowledge. Tacit knowledge is relatively immobile, whereas codified, freely available knowledge can be transferred independently of its location without any additional costs (Brenner, 2007). Flows of codified knowledge are easier due to ICT development.

As the result of the highly contextual features and the nature of its transmission mechanisms, knowledge is considered to be spatially sticky and its flows are presumed to appear mostly amongst members of a co-located community (Miguelez et al., 2013). Knowledge spillovers are localized and tend to decay rapidly with transmission across geographic space (Audretsch, 2003). However, what is worth to point out, empirical analyses reveal that knowledge externalities unfold within 300 km or comparable distance ranges, thus it indicates a much larger distance than the face-to-face impact of localized externalities (Bottazzi & Peri, 2003; Greunz, 2003; Moreno et al., 2005).

Spatial proximity does not unambiguously mean that knowledge spillovers would appear as they do not have automatic nature (Boschma & Iammarino, 2009). Boschma (2005) suggests that besides the spatial closeness, other forms of proximity facilitate knowledge spillovers. In line with his considerations, geographical prox-imity may not be determinative in itself but it has a reinforcing power which triggers the other types of proximity: cognitive, organizational, social, and institutional. Empirical results provide evidence on the fact that simultaneously present, different kinds of proximities generate synergic effects on growth (Basile et al., 2012). Moreno et al. (2005), amongst others, have exploited the concept of technological proximity between regions and revealed that cross-regional knowledge externalities flow easily amongst scientists and technicians in highly specialized technological fields, irrespective of their geographical location, due to the fact that they share a specific knowledge background, common jargon, and codes.

Excessively close actors may have little to exchange after a certain number of interactions (Boschma & Frenken, 2010). Innovation processes require the combi-nation of different, although related, complementary pieces of knowledge to be most effective. Hence, combining and recombining local knowledge could make it even-tually redundant and less valuable (Bergman & Maier, 2009).

If the internal networks are strong, whereas external connections to other sources of knowledge are weak, the risk of localism might occur and may lead to 'lock-in' processes (Arthur, 1989). Regional economy that is unable to acquire external knowledge is likely to be less innovative (Fratesi & Senn, 2009). The balance between proximity and heterogeneity is a major challenge of innovation processes (Mattes, 2012). As Neulärdtner and Scherngell (2022) reveal, embedding in inter-regional networks is in general a significant driver for exploitative and explorative modes of knowledge creation.

According to Grillitsch et al. (2018), competitive advantage of a given economy depends not only on local knowledge resources but also on linkages between related entities, which accelerate learning and innovation processes. Moreno and Miguélez (2012) distinguish two patterns of knowledge interactions: an informal, nonintentional, and serendipitous pattern that takes place between agents located in spatial proximity and a formal, intentional, and conscious pattern of linkage formation between actors, irrespective of their geographical location. The second ones are crucial to access external knowledge that would otherwise not be available for a local cluster.

The effective transfer of knowledge and innovation is significantly determined by the absorptive capacity of a given area (Boschma & Frenken, 2010). As discussed by Arrow (1962), absorptive capacity captures the idea that economies may differ regarding their abilities to identify, interpret, and exploit the new knowledge and to adopt new technologies. It is argued that regional innovation potential and knowledge infrastructure, perceived mainly as a complex of universities, research institutes, R&D expenditures and employees, and regional technology policy, is crucial for the innovative performance and growth of the regional economy (Beugelsdijk, 2007). Meeting some preconditions is necessary for a region to benefit from knowledge externalities and to translate knowledge spillovers into innovation and growth (Abreu et al., 2008).

Knowledge is characterized with spatial specificity as its resources in one region differ from that available elsewhere (Roper et al., 2017). According to the innovative milieus approach, a territory is understood as an organization that links companies, institutions, and local populations within a process of economic development. The territorial paradigm takes the differences in innovation potential into account and shows that a territory, as an organization, can generate resources (e.g. know-how, competencies, and capital) and the actors (e.g. companies, innovators, and support institutions) that are necessary for innovation (Crevoisier, 2004). There appears to be an agreement in the economic literature that localized factors shape the rate and direction of knowledge creation, the spatial diffusion of knowledge spillovers, and regional innovation process (Feldman & Kogler, 2010).

The benefits derived from being located close to other economics actors are defined as agglomeration externalities (Rosenthal & Strange, 2004). Agglomeration in one region accelerates growth because it reduces the cost of innovation in that region through externalities due to lower transaction costs. This implies that innovation processes take place in the core region (Martin & Ottaviano, 2001). Agglomeration effects are connected with industrial concentration and specialization leading to intra-industrial externalities (defined as Marshall-Arrow-Romer (MAR) externalities, originating from (Marshall, 1920) contribution and followed by subsequent works by Arrow (1962) and Romer (1986), economic and social diversity leading to cross-sectoral, horizontal spillovers (defined as Jacobs externalities, after Jacobs (1969)), and the intensity of competition (defined as Porter externalities (Porter, 1990; Glaeser et al., 1992)). Additionally, according to Antonelli and Gehringer (2015), the benefits that can be achieved from vertical knowledge externalities add to intra-industrial knowledge externalities. Many empirical studies underline the importance of agglomeration externalities—specifically specialization, diversity, and competition effects that may contribute to innovation, productivity, and regional development (Cortinovis & van Oort, 2015; de Groot et al., 2016; Neffke et al., 2011).

Different types of agglomeration externalities can create various types of benefits for innovation performance. Intra-industrial externalities are expected to induce incremental innovation and process innovation, as the knowledge transfers occur between similar firms producing similar products, and thus they contribute primarily to productivity increases. Jacobs externalities instead, are expected to facilitate particularly radical innovation and product innovation as knowledge flows from different sectors are recombined leading to complete new products or technological processes and thus they contribute to the creation of new markets and employment, rather than productivity increases (Frenken et al., 2007).

## 2.2 Knowledge-Based Foundations of Regional Development

The capacity to generate and implement advances in knowledge and innovation is regarded as the crucial force driving regional development. Recognition of the importance of knowledge in shaping economic development has its origins in the Schumpeterian theories with reference to 'new combinations of knowledge' as the drivers of innovation and entrepreneurship (Schumpeter, 1934). Innovative output is viewed as the product of knowledge inputs in a knowledge production function framework (Griliches, 1979). In Romer's (1990) long-term growth model, an increase in the stock of knowledge results in a proportional increase in the productivity of the knowledge sector. In the knowledge production function the production of new ideas for each region depends upon the stock of knowledge and the level of human resources engaged in innovative activities. As regions are not 'isolated islands', the spatial interaction effects that arise from spatial spillovers of technology should be considered in the regional growth models (Quah, 1996). As knowledge is not easily accessible and its resources are not uniformly distributed across the space, the location of knowledge production and the characteristics of knowledge flows become critical issues in understanding economic growth. The models of knowledge production are considered to hold better for regional units of observation than for enterprises in isolation of spatial context (Audretsch & Feldman, 2004). Region has been found to provide a platform upon which new economic knowledge can be created and commercialized into innovations.

Pivotal role of knowledge diffusion in development processes was initially recognized in the Marshallian externalities approach. Knowledge spillovers are central in endogenous growth models (Grossman & Helpman, 1991; Lucas, 1988; Romer, 1990), in which positive externalities are a common feature of processes of knowledge accumulation. It is considered that the social benefit of knowledge creation is higher than the private benefit of such activity as knowledge is generally non-excludable and imitators have generally no incentives to compensate the innovators for the gained benefits.

Also concepts of the geography of innovation (Audretsch & Feldman, 2004; Feldman & Kogler, 2010; Malecki, 2021) focused on the localized pattern of knowledge spillovers and their role in explaining both the high spatial concentration of economic activity and spatial differences in economic growth. Within the same theoretical framework, new economic geography models (Krugman, 1991) provide the view that the spatial distribution of economic activity is determined by the tension between agglomeration and dispersion forces in the form of immobile factors of production (Redding, 2010). In line with evolutionary thinking, the spatial processes of knowledge creation and distribution are understood as a cumulative, path-dependent, and interactive, whereas new knowledge is expected to be based on related, former sources of knowledge (Balland, 2016).

In regional growth theories, a great emphasis has been put on knowledge as a driving force of development and on the endogenous self-reinforcing mechanisms of knowledge creation. Development is fundamentally dependent on a concentrated organization of the territory, in which a socio-economic and cultural system is embedded (Capello, 2009). Persistence of regional differences in knowledge bases implies that not only innovation is cumulative in nature, as it results from the recombination of existing ideas and localized character of its processes, but also that knowledge developed in one location is often difficult to imitate elsewhere (Balland & Rigby, 2017).

It is argued that dynamics of scientific knowledge is path and place dependent (Heimeriks & Boschma, 2014), and the current research portfolio of a region influences its further capacity to produce knowledge. From evolutionary perspective, the path dependence of knowledge production means that existing scientific knowledge provides the building blocks for further knowledge production (Arthur, 2009). Knowledge production is also place dependent as it is differentiated among locations (Heimeriks & Boschma, 2014). The processes of creation and diffusion of knowledge and innovation are very complex and have a spatial character (Guastella & Timpano, 2016). Uneven spatial distribution of innovation activity is considered to be relevant for emergence and persistence of regional development disparities (Geppert & Stephan, 2008; Meliciani, 2015).

As knowledge is cumulative, characterized by (dynamic) increasing returns, and inevitable in producing new knowledge itself, regions with comparative advantage in generating technological change for growth, are likely to retain a good position (Dosi, 1988). Regions that are less prone to generate knowledge develop the culture of dependency on external sources of knowledge that consequently discourages regional entrepreneurship and innovativeness (Petrov, 2011). It is consistent with the concept of path dependence that is intended to capture the way in which regions set off the mechanisms of self-reinforcement that 'lock-in' particular structures and pathways of development (Martin & Sunley, 2006). According to Vergne and Durand (2010), path dependence can be defined as a property of a stochastic process which occurs under two conditions (contingency and self-reinforcement) and causes 'lock-in' in the absence of exogenous shock. In the relevant literature, three interrelated versions of this concept could be distinguished: path dependence as a technological 'lock-in' (the tendency for particular technological fields to become locked onto a trajectory, even though alternative (and possibly more efficient) technologies are available), as dynamic increasing returns (the development of many phenomena is driven by a process of increasing returns, in which various externalities and learning mechanisms operate to produce positive feedback effects, thereby reinforcing the existing development paths), and as institutional hysteresis (the tendency for formal and informal institutions, social arrangements, and cultural forms to be self-reproducing over time, in part through the very systems of socio-economic action they engender and serve to support) (Martin & Sunley, 2006). In the institutional-evolutionary approach, regions with efficient institutions, formal or informal, are more capable of generating and diffusing knowledge, and consequently achieving faster economic growth (Cortinovis et al., 2017).

Regional growth depends on the amount of innovation activity which is carried out locally, and on the ability to take advantage of external technological achievements (Martin & Ottaviano, 2001). Knowledge spillovers have an important spatial component, as it has been argued that spillovers do not travel easily, so that the performance of an individual region is influenced by its geographical location. The existing evidence reveals that convergence is often confined to groups of geographically contiguous regions (Magrini, 2004) and the ability to receive knowledge spillovers is influenced by distance from the knowledge source (Audretsch & Feldman, 1996). The existence of localized spillovers of technological knowledge plays a significant role in the regional convergence process as the propensity to innovate of each region does depend on that of the surrounding areas and the intensity of the growth spillovers fades significantly with distance (Boschma, 2005; Paci & Pigliaru, 2002). It is widely accepted that spatial effects have an impact on the process of regional growth as contiguous regions tend to grow at similar speeds (Fingleton, 2003; Paci & Pigliaru, 2002). What is worth to point out, the results of prior studies suggest the existence of spatial dependence and positive impact of the knowledge resources in a given region on the growth of other regions, conditional on belonging to the same functional regions (Andersson & Karlsson, 2007).

It is considered that not all knowledge is equally valuable for productivity and economic development. The productivity and growth of a given economy depend on the diversity of its available capabilities, and therefore, development disparities can be explained by differences in economic complexity (Hidalgo & Hausmann, 2009). Complexity is an important qualitative dimension of knowledge that determines the cost and time of knowledge imitation. As empirical results provided by Mewes and Broekel (2020), knowledge complexity has crucial effects on knowledge creation in an economy and determines the regional economic growth.

As revealed by Kijek and Matras-Bolibok (2020) regional TFP is directly affected by knowledge-intensive specialization of the given region (in high-tech manufacturing and knowledge-intensive services). Benefits from specialization and clustering are essential to knowledge-intensive and innovation activities. The New Economic Geography (NEG) paradigm (Krugman, 1998) states that geographical concentration and localized knowledge spillovers shape regional productivity and growth (Ottaviano & Thisse, 2004). According to Kemeny and Storper (2015) regional specialization should positively impact productivity through the three main mechanisms assumptive in the NEG models: sharing of input suppliers, matching of specialized labour demand and supply, and occurrence of technological learning or spillovers effects, especially where innovation involves many different types of actors spread across different organizations. Spatial concentration of economic activities and growth are mutually self-reinforcing processes. The effects of agglomeration externalities according to the product life cycle and the maturity stage of a given area are hypothesized to differentiate the dynamics of regional productivity (Marrocu et al., 2013). It is considered that agglomeration externalities favour regional specialization as economic activities tend to cluster in areas with a strong functional specialization in knowledge-intensive and high-skilled activities (Meliciani & Savona, 2015). Highly specialized and complex outputs are usually produced at relatively few locations and often provide long-run competitive advantage (Hidalgo & Hausmann, 2009; Kogler et al., 2018).

It is worth to point out that the literature concerning regional diversification and specialization is characterized by dichotomy. The question which of them is the main driver of economic growth and innovation has gained the attention of many researchers since the edition of papers by Glaeser et al. (1992) and Henderson et al. (1995) who advocate sectoral diversity and specialization, respectively. However, empirical analysis indicates that the specialization-diversity issue is not an 'either–or' question, as both specialization and diversity matter for innovation and regional economic performance on different geographical levels, for different time periods, over the industry lifecycle, and in different institutional settings. To overcome the impasse in the specialization-diversity debate, the related variety concept was introduced (van Oort et al., 2015) that could serve for newly defined cohesion policies, smart specialization policies, or place-based development strategies.

The vision of knowledge-based regional development is the core of the smart specialization concept that was recommended by the Knowledge for Growth Expert Group commissioned by the EU. It is based on the technology-driven model of place-based strategies that can be pursued with advantage both by regions that are at the scientific and technological frontier, and by those that are less advanced (Foray et al., 2009). Smart specialization strategies adapt bottom-up approach and they are focused on both public and private 'enabling knowledge-based assets', not on particular economic sectors (OECD, 2013). What is worth to point out, smart specialization is diversified specialization and not the same as specialization as known from previous regional development strategies. The goal of smart specialization is not to make the economic structure of regions more specialized (i.e. less diversified), but instead to leverage the existing and identify the hidden opportunities and to create new areas of high value-added activities that will be critical in building regional competitive advantage (Balland & Boschma, 2021). To achieve diversified specialization a region needs to promote new path development basing on technologically more advanced activities that move up the ladder of higher knowledge complexity (Asheim, 2019).

Smart specialization concept is focused on building competitive advantage in research domains and sectors where regions possessed existing strengths and improving those capabilities through diversification into related technologies and industrial sectors (European Commission. Directorate General for Regional Policy, 2012). Aiming at identification of technological assets that comprise the knowledge cores within regions and extension of innovative place-based capabilities, smart specialiszations should contribute to both reduction of competitive overlap with competing regions and to increase in regional synergies (Rigby et al., 2022). Concentration of public investments in the smart specializations platforms is particularly important for regions that are not leaders in any of the major science or technology domains.

## 2.3  Policy Framework of Innovation-Driven Regional Development in the European Union

The European Union (EU) introduced a structural policy, known as Cohesion Policy, to tackle with the economic and social disparities. The main purpose of Cohesion Policy is to reduce differences and provide a harmonized development among regions. The European Regional Development Policy (ERDP) is a part of Cohesion Policy, which is focused on regional development. It should be noted that regional development regarded as regional convergence has been a political objective of EC/EU from the beginning of the integration process (Ares, 2020). One of the main tools of The European Regional Development Policy is the European Regional Development Fund (ERDF). Support for innovation is a key priority for ERDF, since the reduction of innovation gap between regional innovation leaders and moderate innovators should lead to lower productivity disparities.

Since 2000 a transition has been observed from the 'old' to the 'new development paradigm', as reflected in the Structural Funds programming. This coincided with a history-making moment of the preparation for the accession of new Member States, mainly from Central and Eastern Europe. Structural Funds in the 2000–2006 programming period focused on the stimulation of competitiveness by tapping endogenous potentials of regions in the form of intangibles, social capital, and learning capacities. In this period regional development policy, regional research and technological development and innovation (RTDI) strategies and regional innovation system (RIS) approach became synonymous (Pellegrin, 2007). As defined by Autio (1998, p. 135), regional innovation systems are 'essentially social systems, composed of interacting sub-systems; the knowledge application and exploitation subsystem and the knowledge generation and diffusion sub-system'. RIS was expected to contribute to the Lisbon strategy by leveraging both regional and Community competitiveness (De Bruijn & Lagendijk, 2005). To stimulate the development of regional innovation systems (a 'learning' regional economy) and innovation capacities in the less favoured regions, the principle policy tool, known as regional innovation strategy, was financed under the innovative actions of the European Regional Development Fund in the period 2000–2006.[1]

Regional innovation strategies are based on the assumption of giving an impulse to collective social learning and knowledge mobilization by providing regions with a flexible methodological approach to design effective RTDI strategies. Key methodological principles of regional innovation strategy reflect a network perspective of heterogeneous actors instead of a top-down decision-making approach. This means that regional innovation strategy should be integrated and multidisciplinary, demand-led, action-oriented, incremental and cyclical and should promote interregional cooperation and benchmarking (Landabaso et al., 2003). From the normative perspective, the perception of regional innovation strategy as a one-size-fits-all

---

[1] Average cost of regional innovation strategies was 0.5 million Euro and was co-financed in half by EU Commission and the region (Landabaso et al., 2003).

model, i.e. applicable to all regions, including the less advanced ones, is the subject of lively scientific debate (Tödtling & Trippl, 2005). It seems clear that a regional innovation strategy and related policy responses should be tailored to the type of regions (e.g. rural or metropolitan regions) and their specific characteristics (Nauwelaers & Wintjes, 2002), but this strategy does not offer universally practicable indications for policy-makers.

After the Lisbon Agenda was relaunched in 2005, stronger pressure in Cohesion Policy was put on innovation and knowledge as key drivers of competitiveness during the 2007–2013 programming period. Although a targeting of Structural Funds to improve competitiveness may at first glance seem to be contrary to the main objective of Cohesion Policy in terms of the reduction of regional disparities in the European Union, the objectives of competitiveness and cohesion should be regarded as complementary, since they both focus on the effective exploitation of endogenous potentials of regions (Pellegrin, 2007). Lagendijk and Varró (2013) point out that the increasing role of innovation in the Lisbon Agenda and EU policies, including Cohesion Policy, resulted in three distinct trends of policy integration. First, innovation-oriented programmes received higher funding. Second, 'place-based' cluster approach (Barca, 2009) became increasingly important and therefore deserved close attention from the interconnected industrial and regional policies. Third, 'place-based' innovation approaches were incorporated into research policy (Soete, 2009).

According to Foray et al. (2011) some limitations of regional innovation policy during the 2007–2013 programming period were linked to the policy dogma that not favouring any particular sector or technology based on certain priorities is the best choice for policy-makers. Moreover, regional innovation policies are affected by the innovation paradox, which is that less advanced regions have a significantly lower capacity than core regions to use, in an effective way, policy tools designed for improving their innovation potential (Oughton et al., 2002). It results in a further widening of the gap between lagging regions and regions at the frontier of research and innovation. In response to this situation, regional innovation policy in the 2014–2020 programming period was based on the concept of smart specialization, which situated the place-based approach, related variety, revealed competitive advantage and entrepreneurial discovery as four key priority-setting rationales (Hassink, 2020). Research and innovation strategy for smart specialization strategy (RIS3) tries to bring together a sectoral perspective with a spatial context, linking the EU's Innovation Union strategy that forms part of Europe 2020 strategy for smart, sustainable, and inclusive growth with Cohesion Policy (McCann & Ortega-Argilés, 2015). Over the programming period 2014–2020, developing a RIS3 was a requirement to obtain funding from the European Regional Development Fund.

Table 2.1 presents the evolution of rationale of the European Regional Development Policy towards innovation-driven regional development during three programming periods. From 2000 onwards, the Lisbon Agenda, effectively succeeded by the Europe 2020 strategy, oriented the ERDP towards productivity and economic growth by stimulating innovation activities, in particular within the scope of the ERDF. Over the 2000–2006 programming period, ERDF funds for innovation and

**Table 2.1** Evolution of rationale of the European Regional Development Policy (Ares, 2020, p. 95)

| Periods | Objectives |
|---|---|
| 2000–2006 | Effectiveness<br>Growth, jobs and innovation in line with EU's priorities set out in the Lisbon strategy |
| 2007–2013 | EU investments profitability, results<br>Growth, jobs and innovation in line with EU's priorities set out in the Lisbon strategy |
| 2014–2020 | EU investments profitability, results<br>Goals of the Europe 2020 Strategy: smart, sustainable, and inclusive growth<br>Innovation-driven regional development |

R&D were equally divided between three initiatives, i.e. (1) research projects located at universities and research institutes, (2) innovation means, such as knowledge and technology transfer, and (3) RTDI infrastructure in the form of buildings, laboratories, and business incubators. Almost two-thirds of innovation-oriented funds were targeted at direct aid, divided nearly in half between research projects and infrastructure investment (Holm-Pedersen et al., 2009). It is worth noting that the overall support for research and technological development and innovation in the 2007–2013 period amounted on average to 17% of the ERDF and Cohesion Fund in line with the Lisbon Strategy and later Europe 2020. Most of the funding going to innovation went to SMEs for the implementation of more technologically advanced methods of production as well as for the introduction of new products, while only 6% of the overall amount of ERDF support available was allocated to research centres or universities (Ciffolilli et al., 2016). To support regional innovation in the 2014–2020 period, the key focus of the ERDF fund was on research and innovation policy for smart specialization strategies used to establish priorities for research and innovation investments. This is reflected in the allocation of more than EUR 40 billion to these priorities within the ERDF fund (Schmidt, 2019).

As regards the effectiveness of the European regional innovation policy, Alecke et al. (2010) sought to estimate the effects of ERDF and federal subsidies for enterprise R&D in East Germany in the period 2000–2006. They found that R&D grants led to additional investments, which supports the legitimacy of public R&D intervention. These findings are partially confirmed by Ferrara et al. (2017) who evaluated the effects of RTDI over the period 1999–2010. Their results suggest that there was a strong and statistically significant impact of the research and innovation policy expenditures on Objective 1 regions (i.e. the least economically developed regions in the EU, which came closer to the levels of innovation-related activities (patent applications per million) performed by economically stronger regions. The findings also suggest that the effect was stronger in the earlier years. This tendency is broadly in line with some studies on convergence in innovation activity. For example Mulas-Granados and Sanz (2008) found both R&D expenditure and patents convergence among European regions in 1990–2002 period. However, more recent studies conducted by Kijek et al. (2022) and Barrios et al. (2019) reveal the existence of club convergence in innovation activity within European regions, which to some extent may reflect a change in the approach to regional innovation policy in terms of tailoring its measures and instruments to specific regional capacities and needs.

# References

Abreu, M., Grinevich, V., Kitson, M., & Savona, M. (2008). *Absorptive capacity and regional patterns of innovation*. Department for Innovation, Universities & Skills. Accessed from http://webarchive.nationalarchives.gov.uk/20100503135839/dius.gov.uk/policies/innovation/white-paper

Alecke, B., Blien, U., Frieg, L., Otto, A., & Untiedt, G. (2010). *Ex post evaluation of Cohesion Policy programmes 2000–2006 financed by the European Regional Development Fund, Work Package 6c: Enterprise support - An exploratory study using counterfactual methods on available data from Germany; Final Report* [Working paper]. Accessed from https://fis.uni-bamberg.de/handle/uniba/39281

Andersson, M., & Karlsson, C. (2007). Knowledge in regional economic growth—The role of knowledge accessibility. *Industry and Innovation, 14*(2), 129–149. https://doi.org/10.1080/13662710701252450

Antonelli, C., & Colombelli, A. (2017). The locus of knowledge externalities and the cost of knowledge. *Regional Studies, 51*(8), 1151–1164. https://doi.org/10.1080/00343404.2017.1331294

Antonelli, C., & Gehringer, A. (2015). Knowledge externalities and demand pull: The European evidence. *Economic Systems, 39*(4), 608–631. https://doi.org/10.1016/j.ecosys.2015.03.001

Ares, C. (2020). EU regional development policy, from regional convergence to development through innovation. In M. González-López & B. T. Asheim (Eds.), *Regions and innovation policies in Europe* (pp. 92–112). Edward Elgar. Accessed from https://www.elgaronline.com/view/edcoll/9781789904154/9781789904154.00010.xml

Arrow, K. (1962). Economic welfare and the allocation of resources for invention. In *The rate and direction of inventive activity: Economic and social factors* (pp. 609–626). Princeton University Press. Accessed from https://www.nber.org/books-and-chapters/rate-and-direction-inventive-activity-economic-and-social-factors/economic-welfare-and-allocation-resources-invention

Arthur, W. B. (1989). Competing technologies, increasing returns, and lock-in by historical events. *The Economic Journal, 99*(394), 116–131. https://doi.org/10.2307/2234208

Arthur, W. B. (2009). *The nature of technology: What it is and how it evolves*. Simon & Schuster.

Asheim, B. T. (2019). Smart specialisation, innovation policy and regional innovation systems: What about new path development in less innovative regions? *Innovation: The European Journal of Social Science Research, 32*(1), 8–25. https://doi.org/10.1080/13511610.2018.1491001

Audretsch, D. B. (1998). Agglomeration and the location of innovative activity. *Oxford Review of Economic Policy, 14*(2), 18–29.

Audretsch, D. B. (2003). Innovation and spatial externalities. *International Regional Science Review, 26*(2), 167–174.

Audretsch, D. B., & Feldman, M. P. (1996). Innovative clusters and the industry life cycle. *Review of Industrial Organization, 11*(2), 253–273. https://doi.org/10.1007/BF00157670

Audretsch, D. B., & Feldman, M. P. (2004). *Knowledge spillovers and the geography of innovation* (pp. 2713–2739). Elsevier.

Autio, E. (1998). Evaluation of RTD in regional systems of innovation. *European Planning Studies, 6*(2), 131–140. https://doi.org/10.1080/09654319808720451

Balland, P. -A. (2016). Relatedness and the geography of innovation. In *Handbook on the geographies of innovation* (pp. 127–141). Edward Elgar.

Balland, P.-A., & Boschma, R. (2021). Complementary interregional linkages and smart special-isation: An empirical study on European regions. *Regional Studies, 55*(6), 1059–1070. https://doi.org/10.1080/00343404.2020.1861240

Balland, P.-A., & Rigby, D. (2017). The geography of complex knowledge. *Economic Geography, 93*(1), 1–23. https://doi.org/10.1080/00130095.2016.1205947

Barca, F. (2009). *An agenda for the reformed cohesion policy.* Report to the Commissioner for Regional Policy.

Barrios, C., Flores, E., & Martínez, M. Á. (2019). Club convergence in innovation activity across European regions. *Papers in Regional Science, 98*(4), 1545–1565. https://doi.org/10.1111/pirs.12429

Basile, R., Capello, R., & Caragliu, A. (2012). Technological interdependence and regional growth in Europe: Proximity and synergy in knowledge spillovers. *Papers in Regional Science, 91*(4), 697–722.

Becattini, G. (2002). Industrial sectors and industrial districts: Tools for industrial analysis. *European Planning Studies, 10*(4), 483–493. https://doi.org/10.1080/09654310220130194

Bell, G. G. (2005). Clusters, networks, and firm innovativeness. *Strategic Management Journal, 26*(3), 287–295. https://doi.org/10.1002/smj.448

Bergman, E. M., & Maier, G. (2009). Network central: Regional positioning for innovative advantage. *The Annals of Regional Science, 43*(3), 615–644. https://doi.org/10.1007/s00168-008-0251-x

Beugelsdijk, S. (2007). The regional environment and a firm's innovative performance: A plea for a multilevel interactionist approach. *Economic Geography, 83*(2), 181–199. https://doi.org/10.1111/j.1944-8287.2007.tb00342.x

Boekema, F. W. M., Bakkers, S., & Rutten, R. A. (2000). Introduction to learning regions. A new issue for regional analysis? In F. W. M. Boekema, S. Bakkers, & R. A. Rutten (Eds.), *Knowledge, innovation and economic growth. The theory and practice of learning regions* (pp. 3–17). Edwar Elgar. https://repository.ubn.ru.nl/handle/2066/187416

Boix, R., & Galletto, V. (2009). Innovation and industrial districts: A first approach to the measurement and determinants of the I-district effect. *Regional Studies, 43*(9), 1117–1133. https://doi.org/10.1080/00343400801932342

Boix, R., Galletto, V., & Sforzi, F. (2018). Pathways of innovation: The I-district effect revisited. In *Advances in spatial science* (pp. 25–46). Springer.

Boix-Domenech, R., Galletto, V., & Sforzi, F. (2019). Place-based innovation in industrial districts: The long-term evolution of the iMID effect in Spain (1991–2014). *European Planning Studies, 27*(10), 1940–1958. https://doi.org/10.1080/09654313.2019.1588861

Boschma, R. (2005). Proximity and innovation: A critical assessment. *Regional Studies, 39*(1), 61–74. https://doi.org/10.1080/0034340052000320887

Boschma, R., & Frenken, K. (2010). The spatial evolution of innovation networks: A proximity perspective. In *The handbook of evolutionary economic geography.* Accessed from https://www.elgaronline.com/view/edcoll/9781847204912/9781847204912.00012.xml

Boschma, R., & Iammarino, S. (2009). Related variety, trade linkages, and regional growth in Italy. *Economic Geography, 85*(3), 289–311. https://doi.org/10.1111/j.1944-8287.2009.01034.x

Bottazzi, L., & Peri, G. (2003). Innovation and spillovers in regions: Evidence from European patent data. *European Economic Review, 47*(4), 687–710.

Brenner, T. (2007). Local knowledge resources and knowledge flows. *Industry & Innovation, 14*(2), 121–128. https://doi.org/10.1080/13662710701252310

Breschi, S., & Lissoni, F. (2001). Knowledge spillovers and local innovation systems: A critical survey. *Industrial and Corporate Change, 10*(4), 975–1005.

Breschi, S., & Malerba, F. (2005). *Clusters, networks, and innovation.* Oxford University Press.

Cainelli, G. (2008). Spatial agglomeration, technological innovations, and firm productivity: Evidence from Italian industrial districts. *Growth and Change, 39*(3), 414–435. https://doi.org/10.1111/j.1468-2257.2008.00432.x

Cainelli, G., & De Liso, N. (2005). Innovation in industrial districts: Evidence from Italy. *Industry and Innovation, 12*(3), 383–398. https://doi.org/10.1080/13662710500195991

Camagni, R., & Capello, R. (2002). Milieux Innovateurs and collective learning: From concepts to measurement. In Z. J. Acs, H. L. F. de Groot, & P. Nijkamp (Eds.), *The emergence of the knowledge economy: A regional perspective* (pp. 15–45). Springer. https://doi.org/10.1007/978-3-540-24823-1_2

Capello, R. (1998, September 28). *Collective learning in a milieu approach: Conceptual elements and empirical evidence from Italy.* In 38th Congress of the European Regional Science Association: Europe Quo Va-dis? - Regional Questions at the Turn of the Century.

Capello, R. (2009). Regional growth and local development theories: Conceptual evolution over fifty years of regional science. *Géographie, économie, société, 11*(1), 9–21.

Ciffolilli, A., Sanoussi, F., Naldini, A., Ward, T., Wolleb, E., Fornoni, R., Pompili, M., Liberati, F., & Greunz, L. (2016). *Ex post evaluation of cohesion policy programmes 2007-2013, focusing on the European Regional Development Fund (ERDF) and the Cohesion Fund (CF): WP1: synthesis report.* Directorate-General for Regional and Urban Policy Publication Office. Accessed from https://data.europa.eu/doi/10.2776/056572

Cooke, P. (2008). Regional innovation systems: Origin of the species. *International Journal of Technological Learning, Innovation and Development, 1*, 393–409. https://doi.org/10.1504/IJTLID.2008.019980

Cortinovis, N., & van Oort, F. (2015). Variety, economic growth and knowledge intensity of European regions: A spatial panel analysis. *The Annals of Regional Science, 55*(1), 7–32. https://doi.org/10.1007/s00168-015-0680-2

Cortinovis, N., Xiao, J., Boschma, R., & van Oort, F. G. (2017). Quality of government and social capital as drivers of regional diversification in Europe. *Journal of Economic Geography, 17*(6), 1179–1208.

Crevoisier, O. (2004). The innovative milieus approach: Toward a territorialized understanding of the economy? *Economic Geography, 80*(4), 367–379. https://doi.org/10.1111/j.1944-8287.2004.tb00243.x

De Bruijn, P., & Lagendijk, A. (2005). Regional innovation systems in the Lisbon strategy. *European Planning Studies, 13*(8), 1153–1172. https://doi.org/10.1080/09654310500336519

de Groot, H. L. F., Poot, J., & Smit, M. J. (2016). Which agglomeration externalities matter most and why? *Journal of Economic Surveys, 30*(4), 756–782. https://doi.org/10.1111/joes.12112

Dosi, G. (1988). Sources, procedures, and microeconomic effects of innovation. *Journal of Economic Literature, 26*(3), 1120–1171.

European Commission. Directorate General for Regional Policy. (2012). *Guide to research and innovation strategies for smart specialisation (RIS 3).* Publications Office of the European Union. Accessed from https://data.europa.eu/doi/10.2776/65746

Feldman, M. P., & Kogler, D. F. (2010). Stylized facts in the geography of innovation. In B. H. Hall & N. Rosenberg (Eds.), *Handbook of the economics of innovation* (Vol. 1, pp. 381–410). Elsevier.

Ferrara, A. R., McCann, P., Pellegrini, G., Stelder, D., & Terribile, F. (2017). Assessing the impacts of cohesion policy on EU regions: A non-parametric analysis on interventions promoting research and innovation and transport accessibility. *Papers in Regional Science, 96*(4), 817–841. https://doi.org/10.1111/pirs.12234

Fingleton, B. (2003). European regional growth. In *Advances in spatial science.* Springer. https://doi.org/10.1007/978-3-662-07136-6.

Florida, R. (1995). Toward the learning region. *Futures, 27*(5), 527–536. https://doi.org/10.1016/0016-3287(95)00021-N

Foray, D., David, P. A., & Hall, B. (2009). Smart specialisation – The concept. *Knowledge Economists Policy Brief, 9*, 5.

Foray, D., David, P. A., & Hall, B. H. (Eds.). (2011). *Smart specialisation from academic idea to political instrument, the surprising career of a concept and the difficulties involved in its implementation.* MTEI Working Paper.

Fratesi, U., & Senn, L. (2009). Regional growth, connections and economic modelling: An introduction. In *Advances in spatial science* (pp. 3–27). Springer. Accessed from https://ideas. repec.org/h/spr/adspcp/978-3-540-70924-4_1.html

Freeman, C. (1995). The 'national system of innovation' in historical perspective. *Cambridghrie Journal of Economics, 19*(1), 5–24. https://doi.org/10.1093/oxfordjournals.cje.a035309

Frenken, K., Van Oort, F., & Verburg, T. (2007). Related variety, unrelated variety and regional economic growth. *Regional Studies, 41*(5), 685–697. https://doi.org/10.1080/00343400601120296

Geppert, K., & Stephan, A. (2008). Regional disparities in the European Union: Convergence and agglomeration. *Papers in Regional Science, 87*(2), 193–217. https://doi.org/10.1111/j.1435-5957.2007.00161.x

Glaeser, E., Kallal, H. D., Scheinkman, J., & Shleifer, A. (1992). Growth in cities. *Journal of Political Economy, 100*(6), 1126–1152.

Greunz, L. (2003). Geographically and technologically mediated knowledge spillovers between European regions. *The Annals of Regional Science, 37*(4), 657–680. https://doi.org/10.1007/s00168-003-0131-3

Griliches, Z. (1979). Issues in assessing the contribution of R&D to productivity growth. *Bell Journal of Economics, 10*, 92–116.

Griliches, Z. (1992). The search for R&D spillovers. *Scandinavian Journal of Economics, 94*, 29–47. https://doi.org/10.3386/w3768

Grillitsch, M., Asheim, B., & Trippl, M. (2018). Unrelated knowledge combinations: The unexplored potential for regional industrial path development. *Cambridge Journal of Regions, Economy and Society, 11*(2), 257–274. https://doi.org/10.1093/cjres/rsy012

Grossman, G. M., & Helpman, E. (1991). Trade, knowledge spillovers, and growth. *European Economic Review, 35*(2), 517–526. https://doi.org/10.1016/0014-2921(91)90153-A

Guastella, G., & Timpano, F. (2016). Knowledge, innovation, agglomeration and regional convergence in the EU: Motivating place-based regional intervention. *Review of Regional Research, 36*(2), 121–143. https://doi.org/10.1007/s10037-015-0104-x

Hassink, R. (2005). How to unlock regional economies from path dependency? From learning region to learning cluster. *European Planning Studies, 13*(4), 521–535. https://doi.org/10.1080/09654310500107134

Hassink, R. (2020). Advancing place-based regional innovation policies. In M. González-López & B. T. Asheim (Eds.), *Regions and innovation policies in Europe* (pp. 30–45). Edward Elgar. Accessed from https://www.elgaronline.com/view/edcoll/9781789904154/9781789904154.00007.xml

Heimeriks, G., & Boschma, R. (2014). The path- and place-dependent nature of scientific knowledge production in biotech 1986–2008. *Journal of Economic Geography, 14*(2), 339–364. https://doi.org/10.1093/jeg/lbs052

Henderson, V., Kuncoro, A., & Turner, M. (1995). Industrial development in cities. *Journal of Political Economy, 103*(5), 1067–1090. https://doi.org/10.1086/262013

Hidalgo, C. A., & Hausmann, R. (2009). The building blocks of economic complexity. *Proceedings of the National Academy of Sciences, 106*(26), 10570–10575. https://doi.org/10.1073/pnas.0900943106

Höglund, L., & Linton, G. (2018). Smart specialization in regional innovation systems: A quadruple helix perspective. *R&D Management, 48*(1), 60–72. https://doi.org/10.1111/radm.12306

Holm-Pedersen, M., Millard, J., & Pedersen, K. (2009). *Ex post evaluation of cohesion policy programmes 2000-2006 co-financed by the ERDF (objectives 1 and 2) work package 6a: enterprise and innovation*. Danish Technological Institute.

Jacobs, J. (1969). *The economy of cities*. Random House.

Karlsson, C., & Gråsjö, U. (2014). Knowledge flows, knowledge externalities, and regional economic development. In M. M. Fischer & P. Nijkamp (Eds.), *Handbook of regional science*. Springer.

Kemeny, T., & Storper, M. (2015). Is specialization good for regional economic development? *Regional Studies, 49*(6), 1003–1018. https://doi.org/10.1080/00343404.2014.899691

Kijek, T., & Matras-Bolibok, A. (2020). Knowledge-intensive specialisation and total factor productivity (TFP) in the EU regional scope. *Acta Universitatis Agriculturae et Silviculturae Mendelianae Brunensis, 68*(1), 181–188. https://doi.org/10.11118/actaun202068010181

Kijek, T., Kijek, A., & Matras-Bolibok, A. (2022). Club convergence in R&D expenditure across European regions. *Sustainability, 14*(2), 832. https://doi.org/10.3390/su14020832

Kogler, D. F., Heimeriks, G., & Leydesdorff, L. (2018). Patent portfolio analysis of cities: Statistics and maps of technological inventiveness. *European Planning Studies, 26*(11), 2256–2278. https://doi.org/10.1080/09654313.2018.1530147

Krugman, P. (1991). Increasing returns and economic geography. *Journal of Political Economy, 99*(3), 483–499. https://doi.org/10.1086/261763

Krugman, P. (1998). What's new about the new economic geography? *Oxford Review of Economic Policy, 14*(2), 7–17. https://doi.org/10.1093/oxrep/14.2.7

Lagendijk, A., & Varró, K. (2013). European innovation policies from RIS to smart specialization: A policy assemblage perspective. In E. G. Carayannis & G. M. Korres (Eds.), *The innovation union in Europe* (pp. 99–120). Edward Elgar. Accessed from https://www.elgaronline.com/view/edcoll/9780857939906/9780857939906.00012.xml

Landabaso, M., Oughton, C., & Morgan, K. (2003). Learning regions in Europe: Theory, policy and practice through the RIS experience. In D. V. Gibson, C. Stolp, P. Conceicão, & M. V. Heitor (Eds.), *Systems and policies for the global learning economy* (pp. 79–110). Praeger.

Leydesdorff, L. (2012). The triple helix, quadruple helix, . . ., and an N-tuple of helices: Explanatory models for analyzing the knowledge-based economy? *Journal of the Knowledge Economy, 3*(1), 25–35. https://doi.org/10.1007/s13132-011-0049-4

Leydesdorff, L., & Etzkowitz, H. (1998). The triple helix as a model for innovation studies. *Science and Public Policy, 25*(3), 195–203. https://doi.org/10.1093/spp/25.3.195

Lucas, R. E. (1988). On the mechanics of economic development. *Journal of Monetary Economics, 22*(1), 3–42. https://doi.org/10.1016/0304-3932(88)90168-7

Magrini, S. (2004). Chapter 62—Regional (DI)convergence. In J. V. Henderson & J.-F. Thisse (Eds.), *Handbook of regional and urban economics* (Vol. 4, pp. 2741–2796). Elsevier. https://doi.org/10.1016/S1574-0080(04)80019-1

Malecki, E. J. (2021). The geography of innovation. In M. M. Fischer & P. Nijkamp (Eds.), *Handbook of regional science* (pp. 819–834). Springer. https://doi.org/10.1007/978-3-662-60723-7_22

Marrocu, E., Paci, R., & Usai, S. (2013). Productivity growth in the old and new Europe: The role of agglomeration externalities. *Journal of Regional Science, 53*(3), 418–442.

Marshall, A. (1920). *The principles of economics* (8th ed.). Macmillan. Accessed from https://econpapers.repec.org/bookchap/hayhetboo/marshall1890.htm

Martin, P., & Ottaviano, G. I. P. (2001). Growth and agglomeration. *International Economic Review, 42*(4), 947–968. https://doi.org/10.1111/1468-2354.00141

Martin, R., & Sunley, P. (2006). Path dependence and regional economic evolution. *Journal of Economic Geography, 6*(4), 395–437. https://doi.org/10.1093/jeg/lbl012

Mattes, J. (2012). Dimensions of proximity and knowledge bases: Innovation between spatial and non-spatial factors. *Regional Studies, 46*(8), 1085–1099. https://doi.org/10.1080/00343404.2011.552493

McCann, P., & Ortega-Argilés, R. (2015). Smart specialization, regional growth and applications to European Union cohesion policy. *Regional Studies, 49*(8), 1291–1302. https://doi.org/10.1080/00343404.2013.799769

Meliciani, V. (2015). *Regional disparities in the enlarged European Union: Geography, innovation and structural change*. Routledge. https://doi.org/10.4324/9781315815138

Meliciani, V., & Savona, M. (2015). The determinants of regional specialisation in business services: Agglomeration economies, vertical linkages and innovation. *Journal of Economic Geography, 15*(2), 387–416. https://doi.org/10.1093/jeg/lbt038

Mewes, L., & Broekel, T. (2020). Technological complexity and economic growth of regions. *Research Policy, 2020*, 104156. https://doi.org/10.1016/j.respol.2020.104156

Miguelez, E., Moreno, R., & Surinach, J. (2013). Knowledge networking regions. In R. Capello & C. Lenzi (Eds.), *Territorial patterns of innovation: An inquiry on the knowledge economy in European regions*. Routledge.

Moreno, R., & Miguélez, E. (2012). A relational approach to the geography of innovation: A typology of regions. *Journal of Economic Surveys, 26*(3), 492–516. https://doi.org/10.1111/j.1467-6419.2012.00727.x

Moreno, R., Paci, R., & Usai, S. (2005). Spatial spillovers and innovation activity in European regions. *Environment and Planning A: Economy and Space, 37*(10), 1793–1812. https://doi.org/10.1068/a37341

Morgan, K. (2007). The learning region: Institutions, innovation and regional renewal. *Regional Studies, 41*(1), S147–S159. https://doi.org/10.1080/00343400701232322

Mulas-Granados, C., & Sanz, I. (2008). The dispersion of technology and income in Europe: Evolution and mutual relationship across regions. *Research Policy, 37*(5), 836–848.

Muscio, A. (2006). Patterns of innovation in industrial districts: An empirical analysis. *Industry and Innovation, 13*(3), 291–312. https://doi.org/10.1080/13662710600858860

Nauwelaers, C., & Wintjes, R. (2002). Innovating SMEs and regions: The need for policy intelligence and interactive policies. *Technology Analysis & Strategic Management, 14*(2), 201–215. https://doi.org/10.1080/09537320220133866

Neffke, F., Henning, M., Boschma, R., Lundquist, K.-J., & Olander, L.-O. (2011). The dynamics of agglomeration externalities along the life cycle of industries. *Regional Studies, 45*(1), 49–65. https://doi.org/10.1080/00343401003596307

Neuländtner, M., & Scherngell, T. (2022). R&D networks and their effects on knowledge exploration versus knowledge exploitation: Evidence from a spatial econometric perspective. *Industry and Innovation, 1–32*, 847. https://doi.org/10.1080/13662716.2022.2063110

OECD. (2013). *Innovation-driven growth in regions: The role of smart specialisation*. OECD.

Ottaviano, G., & Thisse, J.-F. (2004). Chapter 58—Agglomeration and economic geography. In J. V. Henderson & J.-F. Thisse (Eds.), *Handbook of regional and urban economics* (Vol. 4, pp. 2563–2608). Elsevier. https://doi.org/10.1016/S1574-0080(04)80015-4

Oughton, C., Landabaso, M., & Morgan, K. (2002). The regional innovation paradox: Innovation policy and industrial policy. *The Journal of Technology Transfer, 27*(1), 97–110. https://doi.org/10.1023/A:1013104805703

Paci, R., & Pigliaru, F. (2002). Technological diffusion, spatial spillovers and regional convergence in Europe. In J. R. Cuadrado-Roura & M. Parellada (Eds.), *Regional convergence in the European Union: Facts, prospects and policies* (pp. 273–292). Springer. https://doi.org/10.1007/978-3-662-04788-0_12

Parra-Requena, G., Ruiz-Ortega, M. J., Garcia-Villaverde, P. M., & Ramírez, F. J. (2020). Innovativeness and performance: The joint effect of relational trust and combinative capability. *European Journal of Innovation Management, 25*(1), 191–213. https://doi.org/10.1108/EJIM-04-2020-0117

Pellegrin, J. (2007). Regional innovation strategies in the EU or a regionalized EU innovation strategy? *Innovation: The European Journal of Social Science Research, 20*(3), 203–221. https://doi.org/10.1080/13511610701707367

Petrov, A. N. (2011). Beyond spillovers: Interrogating innovation and creativity in the peripheries. In H. Bathelt, M. P. Feldman, & D. F. Kogler (Eds.), *Beyond territory. Dynamic geographies of knowledge creation, diffusion and innovation*. Routledge.

Porter, M. E. (1990). *The competitive advantage of nations*. Free Press.

Quah, D. T. (1996). Regional convergence clusters across Europe. *European Economic Review, 40*(3), 951–958. https://doi.org/10.1016/0014-2921(95)00105-0

Redding, S. J. (2010). The empirics of new economic geography. *Journal of Regional Science, 50*(1), 297–311. https://doi.org/10.1111/j.1467-9787.2009.00646.x

Rigby, D. L., Roesler, C., Kogler, D., Boschma, R., & Balland, P.-A. (2022). Do EU regions benefit from smart specialisation principles? *Regional Studies, 0*(0), 1–16. https://doi.org/10.1080/00343404.2022.2032628

Romer, P. M. (1986). Increasing returns and long-run growth. *Journal of Political Economy, 94*(5), 1002–1037.

Romer, P. M. (1990). Endogenous technological change. *Journal of Political Economy, 98*(5), S71–S102.

Roper, S., Vahter, P., & Love, J. H. (2013). Externalities of openness in innovation. *Research Policy, 42*(9), 1544–1554. https://doi.org/10.1016/j.respol.2013.05.006

Roper, S., Love, J. H., & Bonner, K. (2017). Firms' knowledge search and local knowledge externalities in innovation performance. *Research Policy, 46*(1), 43–56. https://doi.org/10.1016/j.respol.2016.10.004

Rosenthal, S., & Strange, W. (2004). Evidence on the nature and sources of agglomeration economies. In J. V. Henderson & J. K. Thisse (Eds.), *Handbook of regional and urban economics* (pp. 2119–2171). Elsevier. Accessed from https://econpapers.repec.org/bookchap/eeeregchp/4-49.htm

Schmidt, J. (2019). *EU cohesion policy: A suitable tool to foster regional innovation? Bertelsmann policy paper, 2019* [other]. Accessed from http://aei.pitt.edu/102430/

Schumpeter, J. A. (1934). *The theory of economic development. An inquiry into profits, capital, credit, interest, and the business cycle.* Harvard University Press.

Sforzi, F. (2015). Rethinking the industrial district: 35 years later. *Investigaciones Regionales - Journal of Regional Research, 32*, 11–29.

Simmie, J. (2005). Critical surveys edited by Stephen Roper innovation and space: A critical review of the literature. *Regional Studies, 39*(6), 789–804. https://doi.org/10.1080/00343400500213671

Soete, L. (2009). *The role of community research policy in the knowledge-based economy. Expert Group Report.* European Commission, Directorate-General for Research.

Storper, M., & Venables, A. J. (2004). Buzz: Face-to-face contact and the urban economy. *Journal of Economic Geography, 4*(4), 351–370.

Tödtling, F., & Trippl, M. (2005). One size fits all?: Towards a differentiated regional innovation policy approach. *Research Policy, 34*(8), 1203–1219.

van Oort, F., de Geus, S., & Dogaru, T. (2015). Related variety and regional economic growth in a cross-section of European urban regions. *European Planning Studies, 23*(6), 1110–1127. https://doi.org/10.1080/09654313.2014.905003

Vergne, J.-P., & Durand, R. (2010). The missing link between the theory and empirics of path dependence: Conceptual clarification, testability issue, and methodological implications. *Journal of Management Studies, 47*(4), 736–759.

# Chapter 3
# Regional Technological Convergence: Patterns and Determinants

## 3.1 Theoretical Background and Types of Convergence

The convergence process is generally regarded as the implication of neoclassical growth theory (Solow, 1956). The assumption of diminishing returns to reproducible capital leads to convergence across countries and regions. Units with relatively lower initial capital to labour ratios experience technology transfers and capital flows from those with higher ratios. As a consequence, the income level converges across countries and regions.

Baumol (1986) and Barro (1991) define convergence as catching-up process in time series of output differences. The deviations between two countries have tendency to narrow over time. If $y_{i,\,t} > y_{j,\,t}$, then

$$E\left(y_{i,t+T} - y_{j,t+T}|I_t\right) < y_{i,t} - y_{j,t} \tag{3.1}$$

for some $T$, where $I_t$ denotes the information set as of time $t$.

There are two key concepts of convergence. The first one assumes that units starting from high level of income exhibit lower income growth than units beginning with low-income levels. Since this process is measured by coefficient of regression, it is named $\beta$-convergence (Barro & Sala-i-Martin, 1992). The second one assumes the decreasing dispersion of income across units. Since the dispersion is measured by standard deviation or coefficient of variation, it is called $\sigma$-convergence.

The existence of $\sigma$-convergence means that dispersion of the cross-sectional distribution of income decreases over time. The faster growth of poorer economies, which implies in $\beta$-convergence process, is showed by negative coefficient of regression between the income growth rate and its initial level, named as the growth-initial level regression. Quah (1993) and Friedman (1994) argued that negative $\beta$ coefficient in growth-initial level regression does not necessarily imply a reduction in dispersion. It is proved that existence of $\beta$-convergence is necessary,

© The Author(s) 2023
T. Kijek et al., *Innovation and Regional Technological Convergence*, SpringerBriefs in Regional Science, https://doi.org/10.1007/978-3-031-24531-2_3

but not sufficient, condition of σ-convergence. This is because random shocks appears during convergence processes between economies.

The studies on convergence initially were based on cross-sectional data. In that case the specification of growth regression includes the initial level of income and the income growth rate between the last and first period. The verification of convergence using this kind of analysis does not confirm the existence of convergence understood as a process. Considering only the first and last period of time interval, ignoring the intermediate periods, can lead to erroneous conclusions. To avoid this problem, the regression for panel data is used. Another advantage of panel data appliance is correction for the omitted variables problem existing in cross-sectional studies (Stock & Watson, 2011).

Another important issue of convergence is the distinction of unconditional and conditional convergence. The unconditional convergence assumes that characteristics of economies, which affect steady-state income levels, are the same for all units. As a result, the growth-initial level regression does not include other explanatory variables besides initial level income. The growth equation in a general form is as follows:

$$\ln\left(\frac{y_{it}}{y_{i,t-1}}\right) = \alpha + \beta \ln\left(y_{i,t-1}\right) + u_{it}, \tag{3.2}$$

where $y_{it}$ is income of the $i$th economy in time $t$, $u_{it}$ has mean zero, finite variance $\sigma_u^2$ and is independent over $t$, and $i$, $\alpha$ and $\beta$ are parameters.

Otherwise, if country-specific characteristics cause differences in steady-state income levels, these factors should be controlled in the regression. The regression augmented with variables, such as rates of physical and human capital accumulation and population growth, has the following form:

$$\ln\left(\frac{y_{it}}{y_{i,t-1}}\right) = \alpha + \beta \ln\left(y_{i,t-1}\right) + \gamma Z_{it} + u_{it}, \tag{3.3}$$

where $Z_{it}$ is a vector of variables affecting the growth rate and $\gamma$ represents a vector of parameters. The negative sign of $\beta$ in the augmented regression indicates the conditional convergence.

The conditional convergence assuming differences in the steady state for each economy is to some extent similar to club convergence. It also does not assume one equilibrium-level for all economies, but it takes a multiple equilibrium for groups of countries. The existence of different equilibria is the effect of sharing the same initial position or other attributes by group of countries. The development of the concept of club convergence can be attributed to Baumol (1986), but its continued formal extension is mainly an outcome of the efforts of Durlauf and Johnson (1995). According to Galor (1996), the difference between conditional convergence and club convergence is that in the case of conditional convergence, regions or countries that are similar in their structural characteristics converge to one another regardless of their initial conditions and in the case of club convergence, not only structural characteristics need to be the same to lead to convergence of countries or regions, but their initial conditions need to be similar as well. Despite the conceptual differences, it is not easy to separate club convergence from conditional convergence empirically (Islam, 2003).

Phillips and Sul (2007, 2009) proposed a procedure that allows to identify convergence clubs. For this purpose, they use time-varying factor model which takes into account individual and transitional heterogeneity. Due to its comprehensive capabilities, this methodology is the most popular tool applied to the analysis of club convergence patterns. The extension of this procedure is the ex-post analysis of the factors influencing clubs formation (Bartkowska & Riedl, 2012).

The other concept of convergence is the consequence of Bernard and Durlauf (1995) convergence definition and focuses on the long-run behaviour of differences in the output across countries. They define convergence in output between countries $i$ and $j$ as equality of the long-term forecast of output for both countries at a fixed time $t$:

$$\lim_{k \to \infty} E\left(y_{i,t+k} - y_{j,t+k} | \mathrm{I}_t\right) = 0, \tag{3.4}$$

where $I_t$ denotes the information set available at time $t$. It means that long-term forecasts of output for each country are equal at fixed time. This definition implies no stochastic trends in the time series of output differences between countries. In the general case, the data are organized in panel form. Then, the subject of analysis are differences between the output of the reference country and each other country in the panel. Alternatively, the average of output for all countries may be treated as a basis (Carlino & Mills, 1993). In the presence of stochastic convergence these differences should follow a zero-mean stationary process. It means that output for all countries tends to evolve along similar equilibrium paths.

Based on stationarity tests, Li and Papell (1999) distinguish between stochastic and deterministic convergence. Trend stationarity of output differences is treated as a weak notion of convergence, i.e. stochastic convergence. Then, linear trend in deterministic component of time series means permanent differences in output levels across countries. Contrary to the weak notion of convergence, Li and Papell (1999) propose its strong definition, called deterministic convergence. In this case the time series of output differences is mean stationary. It does not contain neither deterministic nor stochastic trends. The differences in output are constant over long run. The existence of deterministic convergence implies stochastic convergence, but not the opposite way.

Due to the lack of power of univariate time series unit root tests of the ADF-type to test stochastic convergence, the panel unit root tests are applied (Bernard & Jones, 1996; Evans & Karras, 1996; Salmerón & Romero-Ávila, 2015). There are two groups of these tests. The first one assumes cross-sectional independence between units, and the second one allows for the cross-sectional dependence.

The initial contributions to the convergence literature were made by the papers focusing on the examination of β-convergence. Empirical results of these studies are reported in Table 3.1. The starting point for convergence analyses was the influential study by Baumol (1986). His findings are unambiguous, for the sample of 16 OECD countries, the absolute convergence is present, while for the whole group of 72 counties, there is no absolute convergence. The convergence studies for large groups of countries in most cases show a lack of absolute convergence (Barro, 1991; Durlauf & Johnson, 1995; Mankiw et al., 1992). In turn, for small groups of countries or for regions, such as US states, Japanese prefectures, NUTS regions, the convergence is present (Barro & Sala-i-Martin, 1992; Mankiw et al., 1992; Paci, 1997; Sala-i-Martin, 1996).

The studies on β-convergence using panel data generally confirm absolute and conditional convergence at both national and regional levels (Esposti & Bussoletti, 2008; Islam, 1995; Lee et al., 1997; Maynou et al., 2016; Próchniak & Witkowski, 2013; Young et al., 2008). The exception is Fingleton's (1999) study, which indicates no absolute nor conditional convergence for NUTS regions.

The results of σ-convergence studies are summarized in Table 3.2. Since the presence of β-convergence means the presence of σ-convergence, the studies which find evidence for β-convergence also reveal evidence of σ-convergence (Barro & Sala-i-Martin, 1992; Baumol, 1986; Lee et al., 1997; Sala-i-Martin, 1996). In turn, De Long (1988) and Paci (1997) confirm the absence of both σ- and β-convergence.

Table 3.3 presents the results of selected studies on income club convergence. Starting with Baumol and Wolff (1988), who provide a strong evidence of absolute convergence in the upper income club of countries and weaker evidence of divergence among the lower income countries, several researchers have investigated income club convergence at the national and regional levels. The pioneering work of Durlauf and Johnson (1995) demonstrates complete different results from Baumol and Wolff (1988). Interestingly, Papalia and Bertarelli (2013) reveal the existence of conditional β-convergence with the non-monotonic pattern in the sample, which is similar to the one applied by Durlauf and Johnson (1995). Another important contribution is made by Baumont et al. (2003), who explicitly consider spatial regimes, interpreted as spatial convergence clubs. Recently, some empirical studies on club convergence (e.g. Bartkowska & Riedl, 2012; Cavallaro & Villani, 2021; Lyncker & Thoennessen, 2017) have applied the nonlinear time-varying factor model proposed by Phillips and Sul (2007, 2009). As mentioned previously, this methodology is believed by some authors to be the most appropriate for detecting convergence clusters (Lyncker & Thoennessen, 2017).

## 3.2    Role of TFP in Measuring Technological Convergence

The concept of Total Factor Productivity (TFP) is rooted in the economic growth literature. The conceptual framework of the total factor productivity is based on the existence of the dichotomy between technology and capital formation. In other

**Table 3.1**  Selected studies on income β-convergence

| Author(s) | Sample | Period | Testing method | Findings |
|---|---|---|---|---|
| Cross-sectional data | | | | |
| Baumol (1986) | 16 OECD countries<br>72 countries worldwide | 1870–1979<br>1950–1980 | OLS estimation | Presence of absolute convergence<br>Absence of absolute convergence |
| De Long (1988) | 23 countries | 1870–1979 | OLS estimation | Absence of absolute convergence |
| Barro (1991) | 98 countries worldwide | 1960–1985 | OLS estimation | Absence of absolute convergence, presence of conditional convergence |
| Mankiw et al. (1992) | 98 non-oil-producing countries<br>75 intermediate group of countries<br>22 OECD countries | 1960–1985<br>1960–1985<br>1960–1985 | OLS estimation | Absence of absolute convergence, presence of conditional convergence<br>Absence of absolute convergence, presence of conditional convergence<br>Presence of absolute and conditional convergence |
| Barro and Sala-i-Martin (1992) | 48 US states | 1840–1986 | NLS estimation | Presence of absolute and conditional convergence |
| Durlauf and Johnson (1995) | 121 countries | 1950–1985 | OLS estimation | Absence of absolute convergence, presence of conditional convergence with multiple steady states |
| Sala-i-Martin (1996) | 48 US states<br>47 Japanese prefectures<br>90 regions in 5 Western European countries<br>10 Canadian provinces | 1840–1986<br>1955–1990<br>1950–1990<br>1961–1991 | NLS estimation | Presence of absolute convergence<br>Presence of absolute convergence<br>Presence of absolute convergence<br>Presence of absolute convergence |
| Paci (1997) | 109 northern and southern European regions from 12 countries | 1980–1990 | OLS estimation | Absence of absolute and conditional convergence |
| Panel data | | | | |
| Islam (1995) | 96 non-oil-producing countries<br>74 intermediate group of countries<br>22 OECD countries | 1960–1985<br>1960–1985<br>1960–1985 | LSDV and MD estimation | Presence of conditional convergence<br>Presence of conditional convergence<br>Presence of conditional convergence |

(continued)

**Table 3.1** (continued)

| Author(s) | Sample | Period | Testing method | Findings |
|---|---|---|---|---|
| Lee et al. (1997) | 102 non-oil-producing countries 61 intermediate group of countries 22 OECD countries | 1960–1989 1960–1989 1960–1989 | Exact maximum likelihood estimation | Presence of convergence Presence of convergence Presence of convergence |
| Young et al. (2008) | 50 US states | 1970–1998 | OLS and 3SLS estimation | Presence of absolute and conditional convergence |
| Fingleton (1999) | NUTS 2 regions | 1975–1995 | OLS, NLS, and ML estimation | Absence of absolute and conditional convergence |
| Esposti and Bussoletti (2008) | 206 NUTS 2 regions from EU15 | 1989–2000 | GMM estimation | Presence of absolute and conditional convergence |
| Próchniak and Witkowski (2013) | EU27 countries EU15 countries | 1993–2010 1972–2010 | Blundell and Bond's GMM estimation | Presence of conditional convergence Presence of conditional convergence |
| Maynou et al. (2016) | 174 NUTS 2 regions from 17 Eurozone countries | 1990–2010 | Bayesian estimation | Presence of conditional convergence |

words, the main question for growth economists is how much the output growth should be assigned to the changes in technology and to capital formation, respectively (Hulten, 2000). In the seminal papers by Tinbergen (1942) and Solow (1957) there were first attempts to tie the aggregate production function with TFP. According to the growth accounting methodology suggested by Tinbergen (1942) and elegantly formalized by Solow (1957), TFP can be defined and measured applying a static and dynamic approach. The former regards TFP level as an indicator of 'the state of technology' (Chiang & Wainwright, 2005). Lipsey and Carlaw (2004) define technology, measured by TFP, as technological knowledge that consists of the body of knowledge about product technologies, process technologies, and organizational technologies. All these technologies create economic value (product).

To define Total Factor Productivity, one can use the Cobb-Douglas production function [1] with two inputs:

$$Q = AK^{\alpha}L^{\beta}, \tag{3.5}$$

---

[1]There are more flexible production functions (e.g. the translog production function) that can be used to calculate TFP. However, the Cobb-Douglas production function, due to its advantage of algebraic tractability, is useful to present the conceptual framework of TFP.

**Table 3.2** Selected studies on income σ-convergence

| Author(s) | Sample | Period | Parameter | Findings |
|---|---|---|---|---|
| Baumol (1986) | 16 OECD countries | 1870–1979 | Standard deviation | Presence of convergence |
| De Long (1988) | 23 countries | 1870–1979 | Standard deviation | Absence of convergence |
| Barro and Sala-i-Martin (1991) | 72 regions from 7 European countries | 1950–1985 | Standard deviation | Presence of convergence |
| de la Fuente (1997) | 118 countries 25 OECD countries 16 Western European countries | 1960–1985 1960–1985 1913–1990 | Variance, coefficient of variation | Absence of convergence Presence of convergence in 1960–1975, absence of convergence in 1975–1985 Absence of convergence |
| Lee et al. (1997) | 102 non-oil-producing countries 61 intermediate group of countries 22 OECD countries | 1960–1989 1960–1989 1960–1989 | Variance | Absence of convergence Absence of convergence Presence of convergence |
| Paci (1997) | 109 northern and southern European regions from 12 countries | 1980–1990 | Standard deviation | Absence of convergence |
| Sala-i-Martin (2006) | 138 countries | 1970–2000 | Population-weighted standard deviation | Presence of convergence |

where $Q$—output, $K$—capital, $L$—labour, $A$—technology, $\alpha$—partial elasticity of output with respect to $K$, $\beta$—partial elasticity of output with respect to $L$. For the calculation of TFP level, both sides of production function should be divided by $K^{\alpha}L^{\beta}$. This results in:

$$\text{TFP} = \frac{Q}{K^{\alpha}L^{\beta}} = A. \tag{3.6}$$

Within the dynamic perspective, TFP growth is linked to technical progress (Atella & Quintieri, 2001; Barro, 1999; Young, 1992). Under the assumption of long-run equilibrium of perfect competition (i.e. each input factor is paid the amount of its marginal product) and the constant returns to scale, the measure of Solow residual, i.e. the portion of the growth of output that is not explained by the growth of labour and capital, is:

**Table 3.3**  Selected studies on income club convergence

| Author(s) | Sample | Period | Clubs formation method(s) | Findings |
|---|---|---|---|---|
| Baumol and Wolff (1988) | 72 countries | 1950–1980 | Quadratic regression | Presence of absolute $\beta$-convergence in club of upper income countries<br>Presence of absolute $\beta$-divergence in club of lower income countries |
| Durlauf and Johnson (1995) | 121 countries | 1960–1985 | Regression tree | Presence of conditional $\beta$-convergence in club of low-output economies, club of intermediate-output economies with low literacy rate, and club of intermediate-output economies with low literacy rate<br>Absence of conditional $\beta$-convergence in club of high-output countries |
| Baumont et al. (2003) | 138 European regions | 1980–1995 | Moran scatterplot | Absence of absolute $\beta$-convergence in club of northern regions<br>Presence of absolute $\beta$-convergence in club of southern regions |
| Mora et al. (2005) | 108 regions from the EU 12 territory | 1985–2000 | Threshold regression | Presence of conditional $\beta$-convergence in club of regions with lower specialization in low-tech industries<br>Absence of conditional $\beta$-convergence in club of regions with higher specialization in low-tech industries |
| Bartkowska and Riedl (2012) | 206 Western European NUTS 2 regions | 1990–2002 | Log $t$ test | Presence of conditional convergence in six clubs |
| Papalia and Bertarelli (2013) | 87 countries | 1965–2008 | Mapping analysis | Presence of conditional $\beta$-convergence with the non-monotonic pattern in four clubs |
| Lyncker and Thoennessen (2017) | European NUTS 2 regions | 1990–2002 | Log $t$ test | Presence of conditional convergence in six clubs |
| Cavallaro and Villani (2021) | 27 EU countries | 1995–2018<br>2007–2018 | Log $t$ test | Presence of convergence in three clubs<br>Presence of convergence in five clubs |

$$\frac{\dot{\text{TFP}}}{\text{TFP}} = \frac{\dot{Q}}{Q} - s_k\frac{\dot{K}}{K} - s_L\frac{\dot{L}}{L}, \tag{3.7}$$

where $s_K$—the share of capital in the value of total output, $s_L$—the share of labour in the value of total output. This expression indicates that the Solow residual can be computed directly from prices and quantities. As such, it is an index number in the form of the growth rate of the Divisia index (Hulten, 1973). The main limitation of the Solow approach is that a calibration exercise needs the restrictive assumptions of perfect competition and constant returns to scale, which do not correspond with the real-world economies (Roeger, 1995).

The concentration on TFP levels rather than rates of change is especially important in growth models where technology is the main source for growth and convergence (Benhabib & Spiegel, 2005; Hulten, 2000). From a measurement perspective, the challenge is how to estimate TFP level of a particular country or region. Within a deterministic approach related to the Solow growth theory, Klenow and Rodriguez-Clare (1997) and Hall and Jones (1999) have introduced the methodology, a so-called development accounting, that allows to produce estimates of TFP levels. Among alternative parametric methods, Schatzer et al. (2019) set out the advantages of the panel regression approach (i.e. the fixed-effects approach and the fixed-effects approach with time trend) to obtain the estimates of $A$. In contrast to the cross-section approach and the pooled panel approach, this methodology allows to estimate TFP levels directly without employing the accounting framework.

The recent trends in empirical analysis of TFP reveal a growing attention towards non-parametric approach first proposed by Jorgenson and Nishimizu (1978). Their study paved the way for the Malmquist index, which allows to compare the relative TFP levels (Caves et al., 1982). For two countries (regions), A and B, respectively, with production functions $Q_A = F(K_A, L_A)$ and $Q_B = G(K_B, L_B)$, the Malmquist index is the geometric mean of two ratios. The former informs about the difference in productivity of technology A and technology B at A input's level, i.e. $F(K_A, L_A)/G(K_A, L_A)$. The latter provides the insight into a difference in productivity of technology B and technology A at B input's level, i.e. $F(K_B, L_B)/G(K_B, L_B)$. Moreover, Fare et al. (1994) apply data envelopment analysis (DEA) to set up a widely used distance function approach to calculation and decomposition of the Malmquist productivity index.

Although the Malmquist index is frequently used in the productivity literature, there are different aggregator functions that can be employed to calculate TFP index, i.e. the ratio of an aggregate output $- Q(q)$ to an aggregate input $- X(x)$:

$$\text{TFP} = \frac{Q(q)}{X(x)}. \tag{3.8}$$

Apart from the Malmquist index, TFP indexes include Laspeyres, Paasche, Fischer, Lowe, Hicks-Moorsteen, Törnqvist, and Färe-Primont indexes. It should be noted that the applicability of TFP indexes results from their 'desirable' properties to satisfy certain economic axioms and tests. As expressed recently by O'Donnell (2011) Laspeyres, Paasche, Fischer, Malmquist, Hicks-Moorsteen, and Törnqvist indexes can only be used for making comparisons involving two observations or two time periods, thus they fail the transitivity test. On the other hand, the Färe-Primont index allows to make reliable comparisons involving many objects and time periods. Moreover, it meets all other economically-relevant requirements from the index number theory. Contrary to the TFP indexes implying specific production functions (e.g. the quadratic function form underlying the Fisher index and the translog function form underlying the Törnqvist index), the DEA estimation of the Färe-Primont index does not require specification of locally linear production frontiers.

In line with Islam's (2003) argumentation, TFP level is the closest measure of technology and can be used to study technological convergence. [2] The concept of technological convergence is anchored in the research on income convergence (Hall & Jones, 1999). Conceptually, income convergence may be explained by technological catch-up, when initial TFP differences diminish over time. According to the 'catch-up' hypothesis (Wolf, 1991), convergence in total factor productivity levels results from the fact that countries with lower level of technology than the leading countries should face with more rapid rate of growth in technology. The further away a country (region) is from the technology frontier, the greater the possible benefits the advantage provides.

One of the most frequently provided explanations of the catching-up process is a powerful economic concept of 'advantage of backwardness', introduced by Gerschenkron (1962) and broadly explored in the contemporary literature on technology diffusion (Stephan et al., 2019; Vu & Asongu, 2020). According to this concept, the flow of technical knowledge goes from the technology leaders to the more backward economies. As such, technology is regarded as a quasi-public good that can freely pass international and regional boundaries. Formally, the process of technological catch-up is concisely described in the model of Nelson and Phelps (1966). Rogers (2004) and Vu and Asongu (2020) refer to this model and show that the growth of the country's technology can be described as follows:

$$\frac{\dot{A}(t)}{A(t)} = \varphi(.)\left[\frac{T - A(t)}{A(t)}\right] = \varphi(.)\{[T/A(t)] - 1\}, \tag{3.9}$$

where $T$ refers to the world practice technology and $\varphi$ represents a function describing the country's absorptive capability. The former determines the technology gap. Building on the above equation, the greater the gap $[T/A(t)] - 1$ is, the greater the growth rate of technology the country experiences, holding $\varphi(.)$ constant. In other words, the potential to reduce the country's technology gap is higher when the country is located further from the technology frontier. This is obvious that the increase of the world available technology stock may affect $A$ positively. With the

---

[2]Some conceptual limitations on the use of TFP as a measure of technological knowledge are provided by Ang and Madsen (2011).

**Fig. 3.1** Technology gap
model (Rogers, 2004,
p. 579)

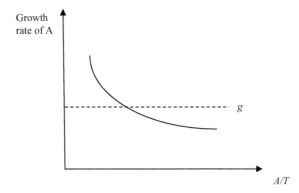

implication of *T* growth at a constant exogenous rate *g*, growth of *A* has to be equal to
*g* in the long run (Fig. 3.1).

As regards the absorptive capability $\varphi(.)$ Dahlman and Nelson (1995, p. 88)
define it as 'the ability to learn and implement the technologies and associated
practices of already developed countries'. In line with Rogers' (2004) argumentation, the absorptive capability is a multifaceted concept and refers to availability of
external technology, ability to learn, and economic, social, and political incentive to
adopt new technologies.

The early empirical works on technological (TFP) convergence was pioneered by
Jorgenson and Nishimizu (1978), who compared relative TFP levels of the aggregate
economies of Japan and the USA, applying a variant of the translog method of
estimating TFP differences. The results show that technological gap between these
countries was reduced significantly during the period 1952–1974. This research was
extended by Christensen et al. (1981), who found that the US' technology was still
ahead of that of Japan. The time series growth accounting approach to test TFP
convergence has been adapted by other researchers, including Wolf (1991), Dollar
and Wolff (1994), Dougherty and Jorgenson (1997), but, as stated by Islam (2003), it
has some limitations linked mainly to detailed time series data availability, especially for large samples.

Apart from the time series growth accounting approach to study TFP convergence, there are many studies employing specific datasets and various methodolo-
gies to capture convergence. Methodological differences in TFP convergence testing
relate to both the TFP calculation method and the convergence type and its verification procedures. Table 3.4 contains selected results of studies on TFP convergence
at the regional and country level. As one would expect, taking into account the
complex nature of convergence processes and methodological issues, these empirical studies produce mixed results, which are strongly affected by the approaches
applied and the periods of analyses. On the other hand, it is worth noting that some
recent studies on TFP convergence apply multifaceted approach. For example Rath
and Akram (2019) study TFP convergence using the notion of stochastic conditional
convergence, σ-convergence and club convergence. Their results suggest that even
in a situation of absolute convergence, there may be different transition paths to the
steady state.

**Table 3.4** Selected studies on TFP convergence

| Author(s) | Sample | Period | Convergence type and testing method | TFP calculation method | Findings |
|---|---|---|---|---|---|
| Dowrick and Nguyen (1989) | 15 OECD countries | 1950–1985 | β-Convergence (cross-section regression) | Growth accounting approach | Presence of convergence |
| Dougherty and Jorgenson (1997) | G7 countries | 1960–1989 | σ-Convergence (coefficient of variation) | Growth accounting approach | Presence of convergence |
| Di Liberto and Usai (2013) | 199 European regions | 1985–2006 | σ-Convergence (Theil index, coefficient of variation) | Panel regression approach | Absence of convergence |
| Tebaldi (2016) | 63 countries | 1960–2011 | Club convergence (the log *t* test) | Tornqvist index | Absence of absolute convergence Presence of club convergence |
| Escribá-Pérez and Murgui-García (2019) | 121 European regions | 1995–2007 | Absolute and conditional β-convergence (cross-section regression) | Development accounting approach | Presence of absolute and conditional convergence |
| Rath and Akram (2019) | 44 developing and 29 developed countries | 1970–2014 | Stochastic conditional convergence (unit root tests), σ-convergence (coefficient of variation), club convergence (the log *t* test) | Tornqvist quality index, welfare-relevant TFP index | Presence of stochastic conditional convergence Presence of σ-convergence Presence of club convergence |
| Kijek and Matras-Bolibok (2020) | 273 European regions | 2010–2016 | Absolute β-convergence (panel regression) | Färe-Primont index | Presence of convergence |

## 3.3 Innovation as a Source of Technological Convergence

The link between innovation and TFP has theoretical foundations in the literature on endogenous growth theory. Contrary to the neoclassical approach pioneered by Solow (1957), endogenous growth theory tries to find ways to endogenize technological change, which is the main driver of long-run economic growth. As such, endogenization of technological progress means that it is explained by the model rather than being regarded as completely exogenous (Jones, 2005). There are a few channels to leverage technological knowledge stock, chief of which are R&D activities generating innovations. It should be noted that R&D-based models of endogenous growth can be generally classified into two generations (Ang & Madsen, 2011).

The first generation of R&D-based endogenous growth models (e.g. Aghion & Howitt, 1992; Grossman & Helpman, 1991; Romer, 1990; Segerstrom et al., 1990) show that TFP growth is positively affected by the R&D levels. The key differential equation of these models is:

$$\dot{A} = H_A A^{\varnothing}, \tag{3.10}$$

where $H_A$ is human capital allocated to research.

In line with the models' supposition of $\varnothing = 1$ the amount of new knowledge ($\dot{A}$) is an increasing function of the existing stock of knowledge ($A$). One of the main reasons of this situation may be the so-called standing on shoulders effect, according to which past inventions make present discoveries easier and more effective. This can be derived from the main assumption of the 'acceleration school' (Machlup, 1962) that each new invention increases the set of possible combinations with huge numbers of current ideas, making further inventions easier. For instance, in the representative R&D-based growth model by Romer (1990), investments in research and development made by profit-maximizing agents lead to the increase of the variety of intermediate goods, which results in productivity growth. In turn, Aghion and Howitt (1992) have introduced the quality ladder model, where vertical innovations in the form of new intermediate goods, which allows to produce the final output more efficiently than before, constitute the underlying source of productivity growth.

The second generation of R&D-based endogenous growth models eliminates the Romer-like knife-edge postulation of scale effects. Within this group of models, there are semi-endogenous growth models and fully endogenous 'Schumpeterian' models (Ha & Howitt, 2007). The former include inter alia the models of Jones (1995a), Kortum (1997), and Segerstrom (1998). These models incorporate diminishing returns to the stock of R&D knowledge ($\varnothing < 0$) to the 'R&D-based' branch of endogenous growth theory. The decrease in R&D returns may result from the so-called fishing out effect, which means that the most evident inventions are introduced in the first place and it is thus difficult to discover the following ones. The fishing out effect is anchored in the 'retardation school' (Machlup, 1962), which in its extreme form assumes that the more inventions have been discovered the less there remains to be invented. The existence of diminishing productivity of R&D activity is highlighted by the fully endogenous 'Schumpeterian' models of Aghion and Howitt (1998), Dinopoulos and Thompson (1998), Peretto (1998), Howitt (1999), and Peretto and Smulders (2002). This is essentially because of the proliferation of R&D effects embodied in intermediate good varieties within many sectors of the economy, which leads to lower productivity of R&D efforts focused on quality improvement. Recently, Peretto (2018) has sought to introduce the new endogenous growth model, in which explosive nature of vertical innovations is balanced by the expansion of horizontal innovations.

Another group of Schumpeterian R&D models focuses on the idea of multiple equilibria in TFP. This group comprises, among others, the model of Howitt (2000) with twin peaks in productivity. A twin-peaked distribution of TFP can be explained by the fact that there are two clubs of countries. The former includes countries with no investments in R&D and with negligible absorptive capacity of external knowledge. These countries stagnate at the lower peak. The latter consists of countries that invest in new technologies and can absorb knowledge from the technological frontier to gradually get closer to the upper peak. The main problem with the model of Howitt (2000) is that it does not distinguish between different strategies for technology creation and catching-up the global technological frontier. For this reason, Howitt and Mayer-Foulkes (2005) proposed an extended model of growth through creative destruction, which implies three peaks in productivity. Countries in the highest club converge to a steady state where they perform leading edge (modern) R&D related to basic and applied research. This R&D strategy needs an appropriate level of human capital, especially creativity skills. In turn, countries in the intermediate club converge to a steady state where they perform experimental development, which requires research and practical experience and allows them to implement technologies developed elsewhere using innovation-effective skills. Finally, countries in the lowest club converge to a stagnation steady state with non-R&D and the erosion of absorptive capacity.

The multimodality of the distribution of TFP can be also explained on the basis of the theory of innovation geography (Feldman & Kogler, 2010). Although there is some scepticism in new economic geography literature concerning the difficulty of measuring knowledge flows that matter for innovation activity (Krugman, 1991), some authors try to incorporate insight from the endogenous growth theory and from the economic geography theory to formalize the interconnections between economic regions in terms of convergence or divergence processes (Alexiadis, 2013). There are some extensions of the first generation of R&D-based endogenous growth models to a two regions framework (Baldwin et al., 2001; Davis, 2009; Yamamoto, 2003). Similar efforts are under way in the extensions of semi-endogenous growth models (Fukuda, 2017) and the fully endogenous 'Schumpeterian' models (Davis & Hashimoto, 2015). These models deal with spatial externalities for knowledge spillovers that affect agglomeration economies for innovation (Bond-Smith, 2021). In line with Feldman's 1994) argumentation, geographic proximity reduces the inherent risk of innovation projects by providing firms with the access to necessary

**Table 3.5**  Innovation and TFP convergence or divergence in theory

| Theory/models | Reasons for divergence | Reasons for convergence |
|---|---|---|
| The first generation of R&D-based endogenous growth models | The constant returns to the stock of R&D knowledge resulting from the standing on shoulders effect may be the reason for TFP divergence. | – |
| The semi-endogenous growth models | – | The decreasing returns to the stock of R&D knowledge resulting from the fishing out effect may be the reason for TFP convergence. |
| The fully endogenous 'Schumpeterian' models | The constant returns to the stock of R&D knowledge resulting from the standing on shoulders effect may be the reason for TFP divergence. | The diminishing productivity of R&D activity may lead to TFP convergence. |
| The multiple equilibria Schumpeterian R&D models | Different strategies for technology creation and adoption induce convergence clubs formation in TFP. Each club converges to a different steady state. | |
| Innovation geography | Since innovation reveals a pronounced bias to cluster spatially, there is a tendency for regions to form TFP clubs. | |

resources accumulated in a region. Moreover, innovative firms tend to form spatial clusters where knowledge externalities allow to reduce the time and costs of innovation processes. Feldman et al. (2002) show how relational networks, initiated and coordinated by research universities, support knowledge spillovers in the form of technology transfer via local linkages and platforms stimulating interactions among firms, individuals, and government institutions.

Table 3.5 summarizes different results on the theoretical prediction of the role of innovation in TFP convergence or divergence. Some theories/models suggest directly or indirectly that investments in innovation may lead to TFP convergence, while others find them resulting in TFP divergence. As regards the scale of production of inventions, TFP convergence or divergence predictions should be considered within the context of so-called 'transitional dynamics'. In this case, the gap in technology levels between high TFP countries/regions (technology leaders) and low-TFP countries/regions (technology laggers) should be expected to narrow and finally disappear during knowledge accumulation due to the decrease in R&D productivity. Contrary conclusions could be drawn for the case when there is an increase in R&D productivity during knowledge accumulation processes. Interpreting the R&D scale assumptions of the first and second R&D-based endogenous growth models and their TFP convergence or TFP divergence implications, it should be noted that these models generally do not discuss the scale effects of technological knowledge accumulation for a multi-country (region) world. They also neglect the key issues of innovation activities such as the existence of different types of innovation strategies and their spatial aspects. Partially, these limitations are mitigated by both the multiple equilibria Schumpeterian R&D models and innovation geography theory that provide theoretical support to the existence of club convergence in TFP. The former emphasize the key role of different strategies for technological investments and dynamics of absorptive capacity in explaining the multimodality of the distribution of TFP. The latter focuses on the tendency for innovation activity to cluster spatially with the principle that innovation benefits most from location.

As regards the empirical verification of theories/models that give support to explain the role of innovation in TFP convergence or divergence, it is noteworthy that Jones (1995b) provides evidence that refutes the first generation of R&D-based theories according to which more R&D staff ought to stimulate more TFP growth. On the other hand, Ang and Madsen (2011) tried to test general validity of the second-generation endogenous growth models. Their results give strong support for the fully endogenous 'Schumpeterian' models and only partial support for the semi-endogenous growth models. Similar findings are presented by other authors (Greasley et al., 2013; Ha & Howitt, 2007). Coming to the issue of the effect of innovation on multimodality in distribution of TFP, the results of empirical research do not allow direct verification of this relation. On the one hand, Henderson et al. (2008) show that a distribution of total factor productivity reveals a tendency to become multimodal over time in the global scope. In turn, there are few empirical studies that deal directly or indirectly with the modality of TFP distribution in the European regions, including that of Di Liberto and Usai (2013), who found that there are TFP leaders separating themselves from low-TFP regions. This finding is partially in line with the bimodality recorded in the EU regional distribution of output per worker by Fotopoulos (2005) and Rogge (2019). On the other hand the existence of two or more peaks in the distribution of the regional TFP can be seen as the result of the existence of technological clubs with different patterns of innovation activity. As shown by Barrios et al. (2019) and Kijek et al. (2022), there is a tendency for clustering in R&D and patent activity in the European regional space.

Another stream of research on TFP convergence and its determinants that relate to innovation/imitation processes directly, corresponds with the aforementioned (Sect. 3.2) technological gap model. In their seminal papers, Griffith et al. (2003, 2004) focus on two faces of R&D. The first one considers the conventional role of inducting innovation. The second one denotes R&D-based absorptive capacity. They found that the greater the gap between an economy's level of technology and the technological frontier, the greater the potential for technologies to be transferred to the non-frontier country via R&D in the sample of 12 OECD countries. This effect of R&D is more important for those countries that are far from the technological frontier. Interestingly, Griffith et al. (2004) also suggest an alternative interpretation of the catching-up process that presumes that there are sharply diminishing returns to R&D. The methodological framework proposed by Griffith et al. (2004) was adapted by Männasoo et al. (2018) who studied the contributions of R&D spending to total factor productivity growth, having regard to convergence processes in the European regions. They show the convergence effect of technology gap, but the effect of R&D expenditures was largely absent in the whole sample. However, a more detailed analysis in the particular subsamples reveals that the marginal return on R&D is reducing in advanced regions, while less productive regions benefit relatively more from increases in R&D. The diminishing returns to R&D is also reported by Burda and Severgnini (2018) who analyzed total factor productivity convergence in the German states.

# References

Aghion, P., & Howitt, P. (1992). A model of growth through creative destruction. *Econometrica, 60*(2), 323–351. https://doi.org/10.2307/2951599

Aghion, P., & Howitt, P. (1998). *Endogenous growth theory*. MIT Press.

Alexiadis, S. (2013). *Convergence clubs and spatial externalities: Models and applications of regional convergence in Europe*. Springer. https://doi.org/10.1007/978-3-642-31626-5

Ang, J. B., & Madsen, J. B. (2011). Can second-generation endogenous growth models explain the productivity trends and knowledge production in the Asian miracle economies? *The Review of Economics and Statistics, 93*(4), 1360–1373. https://doi.org/10.1162/rest_a_00126

Atella, V., & Quintieri, B. (2001). Do R&D expenditures really matter for TFP? *Applied Economics, 33*(11), 1385–1389. https://doi.org/10.1080/00036840010007939

Baldwin, R. E., Martin, P., & Ottaviano, G. I. (2001). Global income divergence, trade and industrialisation: The geography of growth take-offs. *Journal of Economic Growth, 6*, 5–37. https://doi.org/10.1023/A:1009876310544

Barrios, C., Flores, E., & Martínez, M. Á. (2019). Club convergence in innovation activity across European regions. *Papers in Regional Science, 98*(4), 1545–1565. https://doi.org/10.1111/pirs.12429

Barro, R. J. (1991). Economic growth in a cross section of countries. *The Quarterly Journal of Economics, 106*(2), 407–443. https://doi.org/10.2307/2937943

Barro, R. J. (1999). Notes on growth accounting. *Journal of Economic Growth, 4*(2), 119–137. https://doi.org/10.1023/a:1009828704275

Barro, R. J., & Sala-i-Martin, X. (1991). Convergence across states and regions. *Brookings Papers on Economic Activity, 22*(1), 107–182. https://doi.org/10.2307/2534639

Barro, R. J., & Sala-i-Martin, X. (1992). Convergence. *Journal of Political Economy, 100*(2), 223–251. https://doi.org/10.1086/261816

Bartkowska, M., & Riedl, A. (2012). Regional convergence clubs in Europe: Identification and conditioning factors. *Economic Modelling, 29*(1), 22–31. https://doi.org/10.1016/j.econmod.2011.01.013

Baumol, W. J. (1986). Productivity growth, convergence, and welfare: What the Long-run data show. *The American Economic Review, 76*(5), 1072–1085.

Baumol, W. J., & Wolff, E. (1988). Productivity growth, convergence and welfare: A reply. *American Economic Review, 78*(5), 1155–1159.

Baumont, B., Ertur, C., & Le Gallo, J. (2003). Spatial convergence clubs and the European regional growth process, 1980-1995. In B. Fingleton (Ed.), *European regional growth* (pp. 131–158). Springer. https://doi.org/10.1007/978-3-662-07136-6_5

Benhabib, J., & Spiegel, M. M. (2005). Human capital and technology diffusion. In P. Aghion & S. Durlauf (Eds.), *Handbook of economic growth* (Vol. 1, Part A, pp. 935–966). Elsevier. https://doi.org/10.1016/s1574-0684(05)01013-0

Bernard, A. B., & Durlauf, S. N. (1995). Convergence in international output. *Journal of Applied Econometrics, 10*(2), 97–108. https://doi.org/10.1002/jae.3950100202

Bernard, A. B., & Jones, C. I. (1996). Productivity across industries and countries: Time series theory and evidence. *Review of Economics and Statistics, 78*(1), 135–146. https://doi.org/10.2307/2109853

Bond-Smith, S. (2021). The unintended consequences of increasing returns to scale in geographical economics. *Journal of Economic Geography, 21*(5), 653–681. https://doi.org/10.1093/jeg/lbab023

Burda, M. C., & Severgnini, B. (2018). Total factor productivity convergence in German states since reunification: Evidence and explanations. *Journal of Comparative Economics, 46*(1), 192–211. https://doi.org/10.1016/j.jce.2017.04.002

Carlino, G., & Mills, L. O. (1993). Are U.S. regional incomes converging?: A time series analysis. *Journal of Monetary Economics, 32*(2), 335–346. https://doi.org/10.1016/0304-3932(93)90009-5

Cavallaro, E., & Villani, I. (2021). Club convergence in EU countries. *Journal of Economic Integration, 36*(1), 125–161. https://doi.org/10.11130/jei.2021.36.1.125

Caves, D. W., Christensen, L. R., & Diewert, W. E. (1982). The economic theory of index numbers and the measurement of input, output, and productivity. *Econometrica, 50*(6), 1393–1414. https://doi.org/10.2307/1913388

Chiang, A. C., & Wainwright, K. (2005). *Fundamental methods of mathematical economics.* McGraw Hill.

Christensen, L. R., Cummings, D., & Jorgenson, D. W. (1981). Relative productivity levels, 1947–1973: An international comparison. *European Economic Review, 16*(1), 61–94. https://doi.org/10.1016/0014-2921(81)90049-0

Dahlman, C., & Nelson, R. (1995). Social absorption capability, national innovation systems and economic development. In D. H. Perkins & B. H. Koo (Eds.), *Social capability and long-term growth* (pp. 82–122). Macmillan Press. https://doi.org/10.1007/978-1-349-13512-7_5

Davis, C. R. (2009). Interregional knowledge spillovers and occupational choice in a model of free trade and endogenous growth. *Journal of Regional Science, 49*, 855–876. https://doi.org/10.1111/j.1467-9787.2009.00612.x

Davis, C., & Hashimoto, K.-I. (2015). Industry concentration, knowledge diffusion and economic growth without scale effects. *Economica, 82*(328), 769–789. https://doi.org/10.1111/ecca.12129

de la Fuente, A. (1997). The empirics of growth and convergence: A selective review. *Journal of Economic Dynamics and Control, 21*(1), 23–73. https://doi.org/10.1016/0165-1889(95)00925-6

De Long, B. J. (1988). Productivity growth, convergence, and welfare: Comment. *The American Economic Review, 78*(5), 1138–1154.

Di Liberto, A., & Usai, S. (2013). TFP convergence across European regions: A comparative spatial dynamics analysis. In R. Crescenzi & M. Percoco (Eds.), *Geography, institutions and regional economic performance* (Vol. 127, pp. 39–58). Springer. https://doi.org/10.1007/978-3-642-33395-8_3

Dinopoulos, E., & Thompson, P. (1998). Schumpeterian growth without scale effects. *Journal of Economic Growth, 3*(4), 313–335.

Dollar, D., & Wolff, E. N. (1994). Capital intensity and TFP convergence in manufacturing, 1963-1985. In W. J. Baumol, R. R. Nelson, & E. N. Wolff (Eds.), *Convergence of productivity: Cross national studies and historical evidence* (pp. 197–224). Oxford University Press. https://doi.org/10.1007/978-1-349-11786-4_7

Dougherty, C., & Jorgenson, D. W. (1997). There is no silver bullet: Investment and growth in the G7. *National Institute Economic Review, 162*, 57–74. https://doi.org/10.1177/002795019716200105

Dowrick, S., & Nguyen, D.-T. (1989). OECD comparative economic growth 1950–85: Catch-up and convergence. *American Economic Review, 79*(5), 1010–1030.

Durlauf, S. N., & Johnson, P. A. (1995). Multiple regimes and cross-country growth behaviour. *Journal of Applied Econometrics, 10*(4), 365–384. https://doi.org/10.1002/jae.3950100404

Escribá-Pérez, F. J., & Murgui-García, M. J. (2019). Total factor productivity convergence in European regions: The role of sectors and geographical location. *Regional and Sectoral Economic Studies, 19*(1), 29–46.

Esposti, R., & Bussoletti, S. (2008). Impact of objective 1 funds on regional growth convergence in the European Union: A panel-data approach. *Regional Studies, 42*(2), 159–173. https://doi.org/10.1080/00343400601142753

Evans, P., & Karras, G. (1996). Convergence revised. *Journal of Monetary Economics, 37*(2), 249–265. https://doi.org/10.1016/s0304-3932(96)90036-7

Fare, R., Grosskopf, S., Norris, M., & Zhang, Z. (1994). Productivity growth, technical progress, and efficiency change in industrialized countries. *The American Economic Review, 84*(1), 66–83.

Feldman, M. P. (1994). *The geography of innovation.* Kluwer Academic Publishers. https://doi.org/10.1007/978-94-017-3333-5

Feldman, M. P., & Kogler, D. F. (2010). Stylized facts in the geography of innovation. In R. Hall & N. Rosenberg (Eds.), *Handbook of the economics of innovation* (Vol. 1, pp. 381–410). Elsevier. https://doi.org/10.1016/s0169-7218(10)01008-7

Feldman, M., Feller, I., Bercovitz, J., & Burton, R. (2002). Equity and the technology transfer strategies of American research universities. *Management Science, 48*(1), 105–121. https://doi.org/10.1287/mnsc.48.1.105.14276

Fingleton, B. (1999). Estimates of time to economic convergence: An analysis of regions of the European Union. *International Regional Science Review, 22*(1), 5–34. https://doi.org/10.1177/016001769902200102

Fotopoulos, G. (2005). *Twin - Peaks in E.U. regional productivity dynamics: A nonparametric analysis.* Papers on Entrepreneurship, Growth and Public Policy 2005–28, Max Planck Institute of Economics, Entrepreneurship, Growth and Public Policy Group.

Friedman, M. (1994). Do old fallacies ever die? *Journal of Economic Literature, 30*(4), 2129–2132.

Fukuda, K. (2017). The effects of globalization on regional inequality in a model of semi-endogenous growth and footloose capital. *Asia-Pacific Journal of Accounting & Economics, 24*(1–2), 95–105. https://doi.org/10.1080/16081625.2015.1062243

Galor, O. (1996). Convergence? Inference from theoretical models. *Economic Journal, 106*(437), 1056–1069. https://doi.org/10.2307/2235378

Gerschenkron, A. (1962). *Economic backwardness in historical perspective: A book of essays.* Belknap Press of Harvard University Press.

Greasley, D., Madsen, J. B., & Wohar, M. E. (2013). Long-run growth empirics and new challenges for unified theory. *Applied Economics, 45*(28), 3973–3987. https://doi.org/10.1080/00036846.2012.741780

Griffith, R., Redding, S., & Van Reenen, J. (2003). R&D and absorptive capacity: Theory and empirical evidence. *Scandinavian Journal of Economics, 105*(1), 99–118. https://doi.org/10.1111/1467-9442.00007

Griffith, R., Redding, S., & Van Reenen, J. (2004). Mapping the two faces of R&D: Productivity growth in a panel of OECD industries. *Review of Economics and Statistics, 86*(4), 883–895. https://doi.org/10.1162/0034653043125194

Grossman, G. M., & Helpman, E. (1991). *Innovation and growth in the global economy.* MIT Press.

Ha, J., & Howitt, P. (2007). Accounting for trends in productivity and R&D: A Schumpeterian critique of semi endogenous growth theory. *Journal of Money, Credit and Banking, 39*(4), 733–774. https://doi.org/10.1111/j.1538-4616.2007.00045.x

Hall, R. E., & Jones, C. I. (1999). Why do some countries produce so much more output per worker than others? *Quarterly Journal of Economics, 114*(1), 83–116. https://doi.org/10.1162/003355399555954

Henderson, D. J., Parmeter, C. F., & Russell, R. R. (2008). Modes, weighted modes, and calibrated modes: Evidence of clustering using modality tests. *Journal of Applied Econometrics, 23*(5), 607–638. https://doi.org/10.1002/jae.1023

Howitt, P. (1999). Steady endogenous growth with population and R&D inputs growing. *Journal of Political Economy, 107*(4), 715–730. https://doi.org/10.1086/250076

Howitt, P. (2000). Endogenous growth and cross-country income differences. *American Economic Review, 90*(4), 829–846. https://doi.org/10.1257/aer.90.4.829

Howitt, P., & Mayer-Foulkes, D. (2005). R&D, implementation, and stagnation: A Schumpeterian theory of convergence clubs. *Journal of Money, Credit and Banking, 37*(1), 147–177. https://doi.org/10.1353/mcb.2005.0006

Hulten, C. R. (1973). Divisia index numbers. *Econometrica, 41*(6), 1017–1025. https://doi.org/10.2307/1914032

Hulten, C. R. (2000). *Total factor productivity: A short biography.* NBER working papers, 7471. National Bureau of Economic Research. https://doi.org/10.3386/w7471

Islam, N. (1995). Growth empirics: A panel data approach. *The Quarterly Journal of Economics, 110*(4), 1127–1170. https://doi.org/10.2307/2946651

Islam, N. (2003). What we learnt from the convergence debate. *Journal of Economic Surveys, 17*(3), 309–362. https://doi.org/10.1111/1467-6419.00197

Jones, C. I. (1995a). R&D-based models of economic growth. *Journal of Political Economy, 103*(4), 759–784. https://doi.org/10.1086/262002

Jones, C. I. (1995b). Time series tests of endogenous growth models. *Quarterly Journal of Economics, 110*(2), 495–525. https://doi.org/10.2307/2118448

Jones, C. I. (2005). Growth and ideas. In P. Aghion & S. N. Durlauf (Eds.), *Handbook of economic growth* (Vol. 1B, pp. 1063–1111). Elsevier Academic Press. https://doi.org/10.1016/s1574-0684(05)01016-6

Jorgenson, D., & Nishimizu, M. (1978). U.S. and Japanese Economic Growth, 1952-1974. *Economic Journal, 88*(352), 707–726. https://doi.org/10.2307/2231974

Kijek, A., & Matras-Bolibok, A. (2020). Technological convergence across European regions. *Equilibrium Quarterly Journal of Economics and Economic Policy, 15*(2), 295–313. https://doi.org/10.24136/eq.2020.014

Kijek, T., Kijek, A., & Matras-Bolibok, A. (2022). Club convergence in R&D expenditure across European regions. *Sustainability, 14*(2), 832. https://doi.org/10.3390/su14020832

Klenow, P. J., & Rodriguez-Clare, A. (1997). The neoclassical revival in growth economics: Has it gone too far? In B. S. Bernanke & J. J. Rotemberg (Eds.), *NBER macroeconomics annual 1997* (Vol. 12, pp. 73–114). National Bureau of Economic Research. https://doi.org/10.1086/654324

Kortum, S. (1997). Research, patenting, and technological change. *Econometrica, 65*(6), 1389–1419. https://doi.org/10.2307/2171741

Krugman, P. (1991). *Geography and trade.* MIT Press.

Lee, K., Pesaran, M. H., & Smith, R. P. (1997). Growth and convergence in a multicountry empirical stochastic Solow model. *Journal of Applied Econometrics, 12*(4), 357–392. https://doi.org/10.1002/(sici)1099-1255(199707)12:4<357::aid-jae441>3.0.co;2-t

Li, Q., & Papell, D. H. (1999). Convergence of international output: Time series evidence for 16 OECD countries. *International Review of Economics & Finance, 8*(3), 267–280. https://doi.org/10.1016/s1059-0560(99)00020-9

Lipsey, R. G., & Carlaw, K. I. (2004). Total factor productivity and the measurement of technological change. *Canadian Journal of Economics, 37*(4), 1118–1150. https://doi.org/10.1111/j.0008-4085.2004.00263.x

Lyncker, K., & Thoennessen, R. (2017). Regional club convergence in the EU: Evidence from a panel data analysis. *Empirical Economics, 52*(2), 525–553. https://doi.org/10.1007/s00181-016-1096-2

Machlup, F. (1962). The supply of inventors and inventions. In *The rate and direction of inventive activity: Economic and Social factors* (pp. 143–170). National Bureau of economic research. https://doi.org/10.1515/9781400879762-005

Mankiw, N. G., Romer, D., & Weil, D. N. (1992). A contribution to the empirics of economic growth. *Quarterly Journal of Economics, 107*(2), 407–437. https://doi.org/10.2307/2118477

Männasoo, K., Hein, H., & Ruubel, R. (2018). The contributions of human capital, R&D spending and convergence to total factor productivity growth. *Regional Studies, 52*(12), 1598–1611. https://doi.org/10.1080/00343404.2018.1445848

Maynou, L., Saez, M., Kyriacou, A., & Bacaria, J. (2016). The impact of structural and cohesion funds on Eurozone convergence, 1990-2010. *Regional Studies, 50*(7), 1127–1139. https://doi.org/10.1080/00343404.2014.965137

Mora, T., Vaya, E., & Surinach, J. (2005). Specialisation and growth: The detection of European convergence clubs. *Economics Letters, 86*(2), 181–185. https://doi.org/10.1016/j.econlet.2004.07.010

Nelson, R. R., & Phelps, E. S. (1966). Investment in humans, technological diffusion, and economic growth. *American Economic Review, 56*(2), 67–75.

O'Donnell, C. J. (2011). *DPIN 3.0. A program for decomposing productivity index numbers.* University of Queensland.

Paci, R. (1997). More similar and less equal: Economic growth in the European regions. *Review of World Economics, 133*(4), 609–634. https://doi.org/10.1007/bf02707405

Papalia, B. R., & Bertarelli, S. (2013). Nonlinearities in economic growth and club convergence. *Empirical Economics, 44*(3), 1171–1202. https://doi.org/10.1007/s00181-012-0568-2

Peretto, P. (1998). Technological change and population growth. *Journal of Economic Growth, 3*(4), 283–311. https://doi.org/10.1023/A:1009799405456

Peretto, P. F. (2018). Robust endogenous growth. *European Economic Review, 108*, 49–77. https://doi.org/10.1016/j.euroecorev.2018.06.007

Peretto, P., & Smulders, S. (2002). Technological distance, growth and scale effects. *Economic Journal, 112*(481), 603–624. https://doi.org/10.1111/1468-0297.00732

Phillips, P. C. B., & Sul, D. (2007). Transition modeling and econometric convergence tests. *Econometrica, 75*(6), 1771–1855. https://doi.org/10.1111/j.1468-0262.2007.00811.x

Phillips, P. C. B., & Sul, D. (2009). Economic transition and growth. *Journal of Applied Economics, 24*(7), 1153–1185. https://doi.org/10.1002/jae.1080

Próchniak, M., & Witkowski, B. (2013). Time stability of the beta convergence among EU countries: Bayesian model averaging perspective. *Economic Modelling, 30*, 322–333. https://doi.org/10.1016/j.econmod.2012.08.031

Quah, D. (1993). Galton's fallacy and tests of the convergence hypothesis. *Scandinavian Journal of Economics, 95*(4), 427–443. https://doi.org/10.2307/3440905

Rath, B. N., & Akram, V. (2019). A reassessment of total factor productivity convergence: Evidence from cross-country analysis. *Economic Modelling, 82*, 87–98. https://doi.org/10.1016/j.econmod.2019.08.002

Roeger, W. (1995). Can imperfect competition explain the difference between primal and dual productivity measures? Estimates for U.S. manufacturing. *Journal of Political Economy, 103*(2), 316–330. https://doi.org/10.1086/261985

Rogers, M. (2004). Absorptive capability and economic growth: How do countries catchup? *Cambridge Journal of Economics, 28*(4), 577–596. https://doi.org/10.1093/cje/28.4.577

Rogge, N. (2019). Regional productivity growth in the EU since 2000: Something is better than nothing. *Empirical Economics, 56*(2), 423–444. https://doi.org/10.1007/s00181-017-1366-7

Romer, P. M. (1990). Endogenous technological change. *Journal of Political Economy, 98*(5), S71–S102. https://doi.org/10.1086/261725

Sala-i-Martin, X. (1996). Regional cohesion: Evidence and theories of regional growth and convergence. *European Economic Review, 40*(6), 1325–1352. https://doi.org/10.1016/0014-2921(95)00029-1

Sala-i-Martin, X. (2006). The world distribution of income: Falling poverty and . . . convergence, period. *Quarterly Journal of Economics, 121*(2), 351–397. https://doi.org/10.1162/qjec.2006.121.2.351

Salmerón, M. H., & Romero-Ávila, D. (2015). *Convergence in output and its sources among industrialised countries.* SpringerBriefs in Economics, edition 127. Springer. https://doi.org/10.1007/978-3-319-13635-6

Schatzer, T., Siller, M., Walde, J., & Tappeiner, G. (2019). The impact of model choice on estimates of regional TFP. *International Regional Science Review, 42*(1), 98–116. https://doi.org/10.1177/0160017618754311

Segerstrom, P. S. (1998). Endogenous growth without scale effects. *American Economic Review, 88*(5), 1290–1310.

Segerstrom, P. S., Anant, T. C. A., & Dinopoulos, E. (1990). A Schumpeterian model of the product life cycle. *American Economic Review, 80*(5), 1077–1091.

Solow, R. M. (1956). A contribution to the theory of economic growth. *Quarterly Journal of Economics, 70*(1), 65–94. https://doi.org/10.2307/1884513

Solow, R. M. (1957). Technical change and the aggregate production function. *Review of Economics and Statistics, 39*(3), 312–320. https://doi.org/10.2307/1926047

Stephan, A., Bening, C. R., Schmidt, C. R., Schwarz, M., & Hoffmann, V. H. (2019). The role of inter-sectoral knowledge spillovers in technological innovations: The case of lithiumion batteries. *Technological Forecasting and Social Change, 148*(C), 119718. https://doi.org/10.1016/j.techfore.2019.119718

Stock, J. H., & Watson, M. W. (2011). *Introduction to econometrics* (3rd ed.). Pearson.

Tebaldi, E. (2016). The dynamics of total factor productivity and institutions. *Journal of Economic Development, 41*(4), 1–25. https://doi.org/10.35866/caujed.2016.41.4.001

Tinbergen, J. (1942). Zur Theorie der Langfristigen Wirtschaftsentwicklung. *Weltwirtschaftliches Archiv, 55*(1), 511–549.

Vu, K. M., & Asongu, S. (2020). Backwardness advantage and economic growth in the information age: A cross-country empirical study. *Technological Forecasting and Social Change, 159*(C), 120197. https://doi.org/10.1016/j.techfore.2020.120197

Wolf, E. N. (1991). Capital formation and productivity convergence over the long-term. *American Economic Review, 81*, 565–579.

Yamamoto, K. (2003). Agglomeration and growth with innovation in the intermediate goods sector. *Regional Science and Urban Economics, 33*(3), 335–360. https://doi.org/10.1016/s0166-0462(02)00032-7

Young, A. (1992). A tale of two cities: Factor accumulation and technical change in Hong Kong and Singapore. In *NBER macroeconomics annual 1992* (Vol. 7, pp. 13–54). National Bureau of Economic Research. https://doi.org/10.1086/654183

Young, A. T., Higgins, M. J., & Levy, D. (2008). Sigma convergence versus Beta convergence: Evidence from U.S. county-level data. *Journal of Money, Credit and Banking, 40*(5), 1083–1093. https://doi.org/10.1111/j.1538-4616.2008.00148.x

# Chapter 4
# Empirical Analysis of Technological Convergence in the European Regional Area

## 4.1  Data and Methods

The data necessary to compute TFP over 2008–2018 have been retrieved from the Annual Regional Database of the European Commission's Directorate General for Regional and Urban Policy (ARDECO). We use GDP at constant prices as the output variable. The input variables include employment in thousand hours worked and the stock of physical capital. The former is calculated in line with the perpetual inventory method:

$$K_t = (1-\delta)K_{t-1} + \text{GFCF}_t, \qquad (4.1)$$

where $K$ stands for capital stock, $\delta$ stands for the depreciation rate, and *GFCF* stands for gross fixed capital formation. As with (Schatzer et al., 2019b) the depreciation rate is assumed to be 10 percent. The initial capital stock is calculated in accordance with Capello and Lenzi (2015) as the cumulative sum of *GFCF* over the preceding 10-year period from 1998 to 2007.

As regards the data on regional innovation, at the starting point of our analyses we have applied the database stem from Regional Innovation Scoreboard (RIS), which is a regional extension of the European Innovation Scoreboard (EIS). RIS tries to close a huge gap in the access to innovation data at the regional level and allows for comprehensive regional innovation benchmarks. Database includes data at regional level for 21 indicators. The data are normalized using the min-max procedure. Given the scope of our study, we use selected variables that relate to innovation framework characteristics, investments, activities, and impacts (Table 4.1). Moreover, regional data for R&D expenditures in the business sector per GDP and patent applications per GDP over 2008–2018 have been extracted from Eurostat's regional database.

Our sample consists of 219 European regions. The regional coverage of this study is consistent with the Regional Innovation Scoreboard—RIS methodology. Depending on the differences in regional data availability, the sample covers

© The Author(s) 2023
T. Kijek et al., *Innovation and Regional Technological Convergence*, SpringerBriefs in Regional Science, https://doi.org/10.1007/978-3-031-24531-2_4

**Table 4.1** Regional innovation-related variables

| Variable description | Variable name |
|---|---|
| Framework characteristics | |
| Percentage of population aged 25–34 having completed tertiary education | EDU |
| Lifelong learning, the share of population aged 25–64 enrolled in education or training aimed at improving knowledge, skills, and competences | LRN |
| International scientific co-publications per million population | PUB |
| Scientific publications among the top-10% most cited publications worldwide as percentage of total scientific publications of the country | CIT |
| Investments | |
| R&D expenditure in the public sector as a percentage of GDP | PRD |
| R&D expenditure in the business sector as a percentage of GDP | BRD |
| Non-R&D innovation expenditures as a percentage of total turnover | NRD |
| Activities | |
| SMEs introducing product or process innovations as a percentage of all SMEs | PPI |
| Innovative SMEs collaborating with others as a percentage of all SMEs | COL |
| Public-private co-publications per million population | PPP |
| PCT patent applications per billion GDP (in purchasing power standards) | PCT |
| Trademark applications per billion GDP (in purchasing power standards) | TRA |
| Individual design applications per billion GDP (in purchasing power standards) | DES |
| Impacts | |
| Employment in knowledge-intensive activities as a percentage of total employment | EMP |
| Sales of new-to-market and new-to-enterprise product innovations as a percentage of total turnover | SAL |

47 NUTS 1 regions and 172 NUTS 2 regions, including Austria (3 NUTS 1 regions), Belgium (3 NUTS 1 regions), Bulgaria (6 NUTS 2 regions), Croatia (1 NUTS 2 region), Czech Republic (8 NUTS 2 regions), Denmark (5 NUTS 2 regions), France (14 NUTS 1 regions), Finland (1 NUTS 1 region, 4 NUTS 2 regions), Germany (9 NUTS 1 regions, 29 NUTS 2 regions), Greece (1 NUTS 1 region, 12 NUTS 2 regions) Hungary (8 NUTS 2 regions), Italy (21 NUTS 2 regions), Ireland (3 NUTS 2 regions), Lithuania (2 NUTS 2 regions), the Netherlands (12 NUTS 2 regions), Poland (17 NUTS 2 regions), Portugal (2 NUTS 1 regions, 5 NUTS 2 regions), Romania (8 NUTS 2 regions), Spain (2 NUTS 1 regions, 17 NUTS 2 regions), Slovenia (2 NUTS 2 regions), Slovakia (4 NUTS 2 regions), Sweden (8 NUTS 2 regions), and the UK (12 NUTS 1 regions).

As mentioned previously, due to limited access to data on innovation at the regional level, the time period for the analysis ranges from 2008 to 2018. This period seems to be rather short but as argued by Islam (1995b) considering that process getting near to the steady state is essentially unchanged over the period as a whole, convergence-regressions for shorter time spans should reflect the same dynamics. Moreover, the period 2008–2018 appears to be appropriate as it includes the enlargement towards Central and Eastern European countries. Most importantly, it largely covers two programming periods of the EU regional policy: 2007–2013 and 2014–2020, which were geared at improving the economic well-being of regions and avoiding regional disparities.

To calculate TFP, we apply the Färe-Primont index, which meets all economically-relevant axioms and tests from the index number theory, hence it allows us to make both multi-lateral and multi-temporal comparisons. The output-input aggregator functions used for the Färe–Primont index calculation have the following forms (O'Donnell, 2011b):

$$Q(q) = D_0(x_0, q, t_0), \tag{4.2}$$

$$X(x) = D_I(x, q_0, t_0), \tag{4.3}$$

where $x_0$ and $q_0$ are vectors of representative input and output quantities, $t_0$ denotes a representative time period, and $D_0(.)$ and $D_I(.)$ are output and input distance functions.

The aggregator functions allow us to calculate the TFP of the region $i$ in the period $t$:

$$\mathrm{TFP}_{it} = \frac{Q_{it}}{X_{it}}. \tag{4.4}$$

In order to calculate the Färe-Primont index, we employ the DPIN programme. The programme makes use of data envelopment analysis (DEA) linear programmes (LPs) to estimate the production technology and the levels of TFP. DEA is underpinned by the assumption that the output and input distance functions reflecting the technology available in the period $t$ have the following form, respectively:

$$D_0(x_{it}, q_{it}, t) = (q'_{it}\alpha)(\gamma + x'_{it}\beta). \tag{4.5}$$

$$D_I(x_{it}, q_{it}, t) = (x'_{it}\eta)(q'_{it}\phi - \delta). \tag{4.6}$$

DPIN estimates Färe-Primont aggregates by first solving the following variants of linear programmes (O'Donnell, 2011b):

$$D_0(x_0, q_0, t_0)^{-1} = \min_{\alpha, \gamma, \beta}\{\gamma + x'_0\beta : \gamma_l + X'\beta \geq Q'\alpha; q'_0\alpha = 1; \alpha \geq 0; \beta \geq 0\}, \tag{4.7}$$

$$D_I(x_0, q_0, t_0)^{-1} = \min_{\phi, \delta, \eta}\{q'_0\phi - \delta : Q'\phi \leq \gamma_l + X'\eta; x'_0\eta = 1; \phi \geq 0; \eta \geq 0\}, \tag{4.8}$$

Aggregate outputs and inputs are next estimated as:

$$Q_{it} = (q_0'\alpha_0)(\gamma_0 + x_0'\beta_0), \tag{4.9}$$

$$X_{it} = (x_0'\eta_0)(q_0'\phi_0 - \delta_0), \tag{4.10}$$

where $\alpha_0$, $\beta_0$, $\gamma_0$, $\phi_0$, $\delta_0$, and $\eta_0$ solve (4.7) and (4.8).

In our study, we use three approaches to test TFP convergence. The first one applies a unit root test framework and is related to the concept of stochastic convergence. Since the time dimension of our dataset is relatively small, we decided to use the Pesaran (2007) test, which works well also in very small samples (Moscone & Tosetti, 2009). Before carrying out the Pesaran (2007) test, we check the existence of cross-sectional dependencies (CD) in the calculated TFP scores. We use the Pesaran (2004) CD test and the Frees (1995) CD test. The first test is based on the pairwise correlation coefficients of residuals from Augmented Dickey-Fuller (ADF) regressions, where the optimal lag-order is found applying the general-to-specific procedure proposed by Ng and Perron (1995), and is given by:

$$CD = \sqrt{\frac{2T}{N(N-1)}} \sum_{i=1}^{N-1} \sum_{j=i+1}^{N} \widehat{\rho}_{ij}, \tag{4.11}$$

where $\widehat{\rho}_{ij}$ is the sample estimate of the pairwise correlation of the residuals.

It should be noted that the Pesaran (2004) CD test is likely to miss cases of cross-sectional dependence, when the signs of the correlations are alternating. In turn, the Frees (2004) CD test is not subject to this drawback, since it is based on the squared rank correlation coefficients and equals:

$$R_{av}^2 = \frac{2}{N(N-1)} \sum_{i=1}^{N-1} \sum_{j=i+1}^{N} \widehat{r}_{ij}^2, \tag{4.12}$$

where $\widehat{r}_{ij}$ is the sample estimate of the rank correlation coefficient of the residuals.

Pesaran (2007) unit root test augments the standard ADF specification with the cross-section average of lagged levels and first-differences of the individual series. This is done as follows:

$$\Delta y_{it} = a_i + b_i y_{i,t-1} + c_i \bar{y}_{t-1} + d_i \Delta \bar{y}_t + e_{it}, \tag{4.13}$$

where $\Delta y_{it} = y_{it} - y_{i,t-1}$, $\bar{y}_{t-1} = (1/N)\sum_{i=1}^{N} y_{it-1}$, $\bar{y}_t = (1/N)\sum_{i=1}^{N} y_{it}$, $\Delta \bar{y}_t = \bar{y}_t - \bar{y}_{t-1}$ $a_i$, $b_i$,$c_i$, $d_i$ are the parameters and $e_{it}$ is the error term.

The unit root hypothesis relies on the t-ratio of the estimate of $b_i\left(\widehat{b}_i\right)$ in Eq. (3.8). A truncated version of cross-sectionally augmented ADF t-statistics is also taken into account to correct for undue influence of extreme observations in short-T panels. Following the common practice in the time series convergence literature

(Hernández-Salmerón & Romero-Ávila, 2015), our variable of interest for unit root and CD testing is relative TFP levels, i.e. $\text{RTFP}_{it} = \ln\left(\frac{\text{TFP}_{it}}{\overline{\text{TFP}_t}}\right)$.

The second approach is related to the $\beta$-convergence concept. Within this framework a starting-point for further analyses is the Barro-type growth model for panel data setting, which takes the following form:

$$\Delta y_{it} = \beta_0 + \beta_1 y_{i,t-1} + x'_{it}\beta + \gamma_i + \varepsilon_{it}, \tag{4.14}$$

where $\beta_0$ is the constant, $\beta_1$ is the $\beta$-convergence parameter, [1] $\gamma_i$ addresses region-specific fixed effects, $x_{it}$ is a vector of additional regressors, while $\beta$ is a vector that shows their influence on the growth of $y$, and finally $\varepsilon_{it}$ is the error term.

To estimate the parameters of Eq. (4.14), it is transformed into the following form:

$$y_{it} = \beta_0 + (1 + \beta_1)y_{i,t-1} + x'_{it}\beta + \gamma_i + \varepsilon_{it}, \tag{4.15}$$

which allows to use efficient generalized method of moments (GMM) estimators. For datasets with many panels and few periods, like in our case, the system generalized method of moment (GMM-SYS) estimator proposed by Blundell and Bond (1998) is preferred. As shown by Bouayad-Agha-Hamouche and Védrine (2010), this estimator can be successfully incorporated into strategies to estimate dynamic panel models and spatial dynamic panel models used to study regional convergence. To addresses the spatial dimension of convergence processes, we consider the following general specification of the spatial dynamic panel model:

$$y_{it} = \beta_0 + (1 + \beta_1)y_{i,t-1} + \rho W y_{it} + \theta W y_{i,t-1} + x'_{it}\beta + \phi W x'_{it} + \gamma_i \\ + u_{it}, u_{it} = \lambda W u_{it} + \varepsilon_{it}, \tag{4.16}$$

where $\rho$ represents the intensity of a contemporaneous spatial effect of $y$, $\theta$ captures space-time autoregressive dependence of $y$, $\phi$ is a vector that shows spatial effects of additional regressors on $y$, $u_{it}$ is the sum of a spatially weighted average of the error components of neighbouring regions and the common error term, and $W$ is a spatial weight matrix.

In the context of spatial effects of TFP we also calculate the Getis-Ord $G_i^*$ local statistic, which is given as Ord and Getis (1995):

---

[1] Since $\beta = -(1 - e^{-\gamma\tau})$, the implied speed of convergence, i.e. the parameter $\gamma$, is calculated as $\gamma = -\ln(\beta + 1)/\tau$. In our case the time interval $\tau$ is 1 year.

$$G_i^* = \frac{\sum\limits_{j=1}^{N} w_{ij}y_j - \bar{y}\sum\limits_{j=1}^{N} w_{ij}}{s\sqrt{\frac{\left[N\sum\limits_{i=1}^{N} w_{ij}^2 - \left(\sum\limits_{j=1}^{N} w_{ij}\right)^2\right]}{N-1}}}, \tag{4.17}$$

where $y_j$ is the level of $y$ for region $j$, $w_{ij}$ is the weight between feature $i$ and $j$,

$\bar{y} = \sum\limits_{j=1}^{N} y_j$, and $s = \sqrt{\frac{\sum\limits_{j=1}^{N} y_j^2}{N} - \bar{y}^2}$.

The $G_i^*$ statistic is a $z$-score. A high positive $z$-score for a given region shows there is an apparent concentration of high $y$ levels within its neighbourhood of a certain distance (hot spot), while a high negative $z$-score means the clustering of low $y$ levels (cold spot).

Finally, our third approach to regional convergence considers the concept of club convergence. We conduct a twin-path analysis of this kind of convergence. Firstly, we apply the log $t$ test proposed by Phillips and Sul (2007b). The test is based on time-varying factor representation of convergence variable:

$$y_{it} = \delta_{it}\mu_t, \tag{4.18}$$

where $\mu_t$ is common factor and $\delta_{it}$ is time-varying idiosyncratic distance from the common factor. The time-varying element $\delta_{it}$ is modelled in semiparametric form as:

$$\delta_{it} = \delta_i + \sigma_i\xi_{it}L(t)^{-1}t^{-\alpha}, \tag{4.19}$$

where $\delta_i$ is time-invariant part of $\delta_{it}$, $\sigma_i$ is idiosyncratic scale parameter, $\xi_{it}$ is iid(0, 1) across $i$ and weakly dependent over $t$, and $L(t)$ is a slowly varying function for which $L(t) \to \infty$ as $t \to \infty$.

The relative loading coefficient:

$$h_{it} = \frac{y_{it}}{N^{-1}\sum_{i=1}^{N} y_{it}} = \frac{\delta_{it}}{N^{-1}\sum_{i=1}^{N} \delta_{it}} \tag{4.20}$$

measures the relation of loading coefficient $\delta_{it}$ to the panel average at time $t$. As the cross-sectional mean of $h_{it}$ is unity, its variance is given by:

$$H_t = \frac{1}{N}\sum_{i=1}^{N} (h_{it} - 1)^2. \tag{4.21}$$

The convergence is present if $H_t \to \infty$ as $t \to \infty$.

Considering the approach of Phillips and Sul (2007b), the null hypothesis of convergence test is formulated as follows:

$$H_0 = \delta_i = \delta \text{ and } \alpha \geq 0 \text{ against } H_1 : \delta_i \neq \delta \text{ for all } i \text{ or } \alpha < 0.$$

The testing procedure consists of the following steps:

1. Calculation of cross-sectional variance ratios $H_1/H_t$ ($t = 1, 2, \ldots, T$).
2. Estimation of the following regression:

$$\log\left(\frac{H_1}{H_t}\right) - 2\log L(t) = a + b\log t + u_t, \text{ for } t = [rT], [rT] + 1, \ldots, T,$$

where $r \in (0, 1)$. Following the results of their simulations, Phillips and Sul (2007b) recommend the use of $r \in [0.2, 0.3]$. When $T$ is small, $r = 0.2$ is preferred, and if $T$ is large, $r = 0.3$ is better choice.

3. Application of autocorrelation and heteroskedasticity robust one-sided $t$ test to verify null hypothesis $\alpha \geq 0$ using $\hat{b} = 2\hat{a}$ and a HAC standard error. At a standard significance level (0.05), the null hypothesis is rejected if $t_{\hat{b}} < -1.65$.

Rejection of the null hypothesis means that there is no convergence in the group of all panel units. It does not imply, however, that there is no evidence of convergence in sub-groups of units (i.e. club convergence). Phillips and Sul (2009b) propose a specific procedure for testing club convergence. The algorithm includes four steps. First, the units are arranged in descending order with respect to the last period. Next, a core group is formed by adding regions one after another to a group of the two highest-TFP regions at the start and performing the log $t$ test until the $t_{\hat{b}}$ for this group is larger than $-1.65$. Then, the log $t$ test is performed again for this group and all the other units (one after another), forming the sample to find if they converge. If they do not converge, the first three steps are performed for all the other units. In the case that no clubs are identified, it means that those units diverge.

To endogenize the process of clubs formation on the basis of the log $t$ test procedure, an ordered logit model pioneered by McKelvey and Zavoina (1975) is used. This model can be written as:

$$y_i^* = X_i\beta + \varepsilon_i, \tag{4.22}$$

where $y_i^*$ is a latent variable that relates to a region's individual steady-state TFP level, $X_i$ includes the explanatory variables (in the initial period) presented in Table 4.1 as well as a constant term, $\beta$ is a vector that contains the structural coefficients, and $\varepsilon_i$ is the error term that has a logistic distribution.

Secondly, we employ a two-step procedure for club convergence testing. Following the RIS methodology (European Commission, 2021), we create a composite indicator to evaluate regional innovation performance. For this purpose, we use Technique for Order Preference by Similarity to Ideal Solution (TOPSIS). This method takes into account the distances to both the ideal and the negative-ideal solutions concurrently, given the relative closeness to the ideal solution (Hwang & Yoon, 1981). A TOPSIS algorithm includes the following steps: (1) construction of the normalized decision matrix, (2) construction of the weighted normalized decision matrix, (3) determination of the ideal and negative-ideal solutions, (4) calculation of the separation measure, (5) calculation of the relative closeness to the ideal solution, (6) preparation of the preference order ranking. Next, we employ the classification scheme used in the RIS (European Commission, 2021): innovation leaders (all regions with a relative performance more than 125% of the sample average), strong innovators (all regions with a relative performance between 100% and 125% of the sample average), moderate innovators (all regions with a relative performance between 70% and 100% of the sample average) and emerging innovators (all regions with a relative performance below 70% of the sample). Having identified four different sub-groups of regions, we perform the standard Barro-style convergence testing within the clusters.

## 4.2   Spatial Distribution of TFP Across the EU Regions

Figure 4.1 presents the levels of TFP calculated using the Färe-Primont index for 219 European regions in 2008 and 2018. The average value of TFP levels for all the examined regions was equal to 0.242 in 2008 and increased only by 6% during the next 10 years reaching the level of 0.257 in 2018.

As Fig. 4.1 presents, the most productive regions in EU are located along the UK–Germany–Italy corridor both in 2008 and 2018. It is worth to point out that for decades, a banana-shaped metropolitan axis running from London to Milan—dubbed the 'Blue Banana'—has been Europe's major place abounding in innovation and growth (Hospers, 2003).

In 2008, the highest value of TFP occurred in the London region (0.441), and it was 80% higher than the average level for the analyzed NUTS 2 regions and nearly five times higher than the lowest level in the Bulgarian Southern Central region. The second-best score was achieved by the Dutch region of Groningen, and the third one by the German region of Düsseldorf, with the TFP levels equal 0.423 and 0.366, accordingly. What is worth to point, four out of the top ten most productive regions of examined sample were from Germany (besides Düsseldorf–Bremen, Darmstadt and Köln). The lowest levels of TFP were present in peripheral regions of Eastern and South-Eastern Europe. Six out of ten regions with the lowest levels of TFP ranging from 0.10 to 0.142 were Bulgarian and four of them, with the TFP levels ranging from 0.112 to 0.141, were Romanian. Similar findings are reported by Puškárová and Piribauer (2016). The extremely low TFP levels for these regions were also revealed by Beugelsdijk et al. (2018) who, contrary to our methodology, apply the technique of development accounting to find differences in total factor productivity (TFP) in the EU regions.

Although the advantage of the London region has decreased during the examined decade, it has managed to maintain the leading position of the most productive European region. Despite the decline in the TFP level in the London region to 0.440

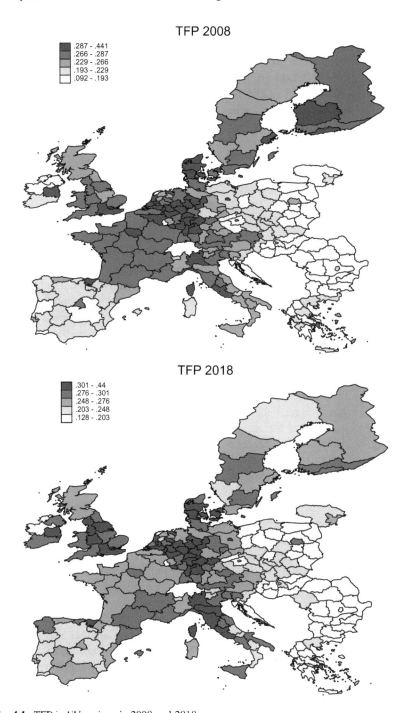

**Fig. 4.1**   TFP in EU regions in 2008 and 2018

in 2018, it was still considerably (70%) higher than medium level for the analyzed NUTS 2 regions and nearly 3.5 times higher than the lowest level in the Bulgarian Southern Central region. The second-best most productive was the Eastern and Midland Region of Ireland with TFP level equal 0.403 in 2018, with the 23% increase from 2010. Half of the top ten most productive European regions was German, as the Arnsberg region has joined the previous best four (Düsseldorf, Bremen, Darmstadt, and Köln). In 2018, the lowest levels of TFP were again observed in the peripheral regions of Eastern and South-Eastern Europe. However, besides the Bulgarian and Romanian regions, the Irish Northern and Western Region, the Polish Podlaskie Voivodship and Greek Western Macedonia appeared among the least productive regions.

During the analyzed period the largest increase in TFP performance (by more than 50%) was recorded in the Portuguese Autonomous Region of Madeira. What is worth to point out, although the Bulgarian regions are among those with the lowest levels of productivity, they achieved the highest increase of TFP levels (by more than 40%). This can be attributable to a low-base effect.

The TFP distribution is also interrelated with urban–rural distribution of specialization levels. Specialization in knowledge-intensive services is found to be the strongest in more densely inhabited areas, i.e. agglomerated regions (Capello & Lenzi, 2013). The observed disparities in TFP performance across the EU regions result, undoubtedly, from the EU enlargement to a set of 28 countries. As in the last decade, old member countries have experienced a six-time slower than the new member countries, which has induced them to delocalize part of their traditional industries to the new ones, they have developed specialization in knowledge-intensive services whereas the new ones in low-tech manufacturing (Marrocu et al., 2013).

As Fig. 4.1 shows, a high degree of dispersion in TFP can be noticed also within the examined countries. To assess the dispersion in TFP, we draw a box-plot showing the variation (i.e. interquartile range) in TFP within each country in 2008 and 2018 (Fig. 4.2).

The box-plot reveals that the degree of variation in TFP varies across countries. In countries like Belgium, Germany, Italy and the Netherlands, where TFP is on average high, there is also a considerable interregional dispersion in TFP. Interpreting the results for Belgium, it should be noted that there are only 3 regions. The low number of regions is also observed in Ireland, which is characterized by high interregional dispersion in TFP. On the other hand, there are examples of large countries, including France, characterized by relatively low levels of interregional dispersion of TFP. In the Eastern and South-Eastern European countries, where the TFP levels are on average low, the distribution of TFP variation is also polarized, with the highest interregional dispersion of TFP in Poland in 2008 and Romania in 2018. The observed considerable interregional dispersion in regional TFP within countries might arise from different efficiency of innovation and regional policies pursued at the national level aimed at reducing interregional disparities.

The spatial clusters of TFP (hot and cold spots) resulted from the local $G_i^*$ statistics for the sample regions in the year 2008 and 2018 are shown in Fig. 4.3.

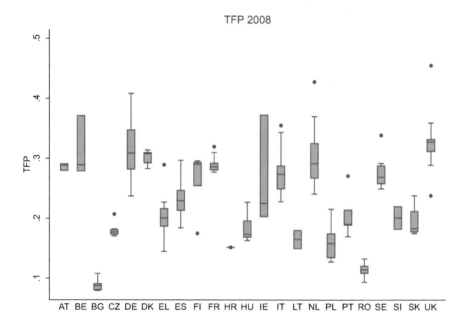

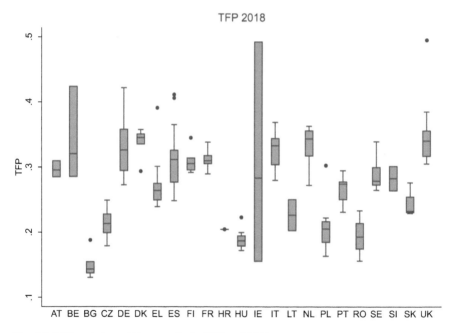

**Fig. 4.2**   TFP variation within countries in 2008 and 2018

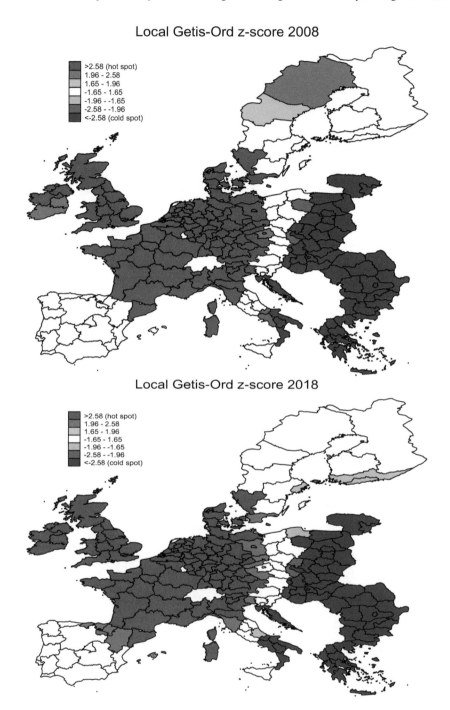

**Fig. 4.3** TFP spatial clusters (hot and cold spots) of European regions in 2008 and 2018

The hot spots, (red colour) mean clusterings of regions with high TFP levels, and the cold spots (blue colour) represent clusterings of regions with low TFP levels. The results of local statistics obtained from the spatial autocorrelation analysis at the beginning of the study period confirm clear east-west and north-south divisions of TFP clustering. There are visible tendencies of the spatial clustering of regions with high TFP in both the west and the north and of low TFP in the east and the south. It is worth pointing out that among the regions concerned, the Spanish and Portuguese regions have less of a tendency to cluster. The same holds true for the regions from Sweden and Finland. As regards the degree of spots polarization, most of the top 10 hot spots are formed by the regions from the Benelux countries (the Netherlands and Belgium). In turn, most of top 10 cold spots are made up of regions belonging to the countries located in the Central and Eastern Europe (Romania and Hungary).

From 2008 to 2018, the pattern of TFP clustering was not significantly altered, but spatial segregation between hot and cold spots slightly increased. It should be noted that the hot spot narrows as spatial clustering is becoming more random in the central part and the northern part of European regional scope at the end of the analyzed period. In the case of cold spots, there is the opposite trend, reflected in the increase of spatial clustering of regions with low TFP levels. This tendency is particularly evident in the regions from Bulgaria and Romania. As regards the polarisations of the spots, the spatial distribution of top 10 hot spots and the top 10 cold spots in 2018 is similar to the distribution observed in 2008.

## 4.3  Analysis of Regional Technological Convergence

In line with the research procedure of our study, as outlined in subhead 4.1, we start with the analysis of stochastic TFP convergence. Since the assumption of cross-sectional independence seems to be unreasonable and is subject to severe critique (Breitung & Pesaran, 2008), we take into account the presence of cross-sectional dependence when carrying out a panel unit root test. In order to check cross-sectional dependence empirically in our panel of TFP for the 219 European regions over the period 2008–2018, we apply the CD statistics of Pesaran (2004) and Frees (1995).

Table 4.2 shows the results of CD tests. Both CD statistics reject the null hypothesis of cross-section independence at $p < 0.000$. These findings are not altered after including a linear trend into the specifications. Hence, a cross-sectional dependence in the analysis of stochastic and deterministic TFP convergence should be allowed.

Our results confirm that interregional cooperation creates the potential to access external knowledge and contributes to increase in the innovation capacity of regions. As innovation processes require the combination of different, although related, complementary pieces of knowledge to be most effective, the access to external knowledge allows to lower the risk of localism and lock-in processes (Arthur, 1989). Embedding in interregional networks of cooperation is in general a significant driver for exploitative and explorative modes of knowledge creation (Neuländtner &

**Table 4.2** Cross-sectional dependence test

| Test | Specification without trend—deterministic convergence | Specification with trend—stochastic convergence |
|---|---|---|
| Pesaran test | | |
| Statistic | 46.599 | 39.494 |
| $p$-value | 0,0.000 | 0,0.000 |
| Frees test | | |
| Statistic | 3.823 | 10.598 |
| Critical values at: | 0.10 | 0.317 |
| | 0.05 | 0.433 |
| | 0.01 | 0.661 |

**Table 4.3** Results of panel unit root test

| Test | Specification without trend—deterministic convergence | Specification with trend—stochastic convergence |
|---|---|---|
| Pesaran test | | |
| Statistic | −1.662 | −4.025 |
| $p$-value | 0.744 | 0.000 |

Scherngell, 2022). Moreover, as Fratesi and Senn (2009) reveal, regional economies that are capable to acquire external knowledge are likely to be more innovative.

Having found the existence of cross-sectional dependence in the panel of TFP, we proceed to study the existence of stochastic convergence by the application of the Pesaran (2007) test. The null hypothesis of this test assumes nonstationarity (i.e. no convergence), the alternative hypothesis assumes stationarity (i.e. convergence). As reported in Table 4.3, the results support the weaker notion of convergence given by stochastic convergence, which allows existence of consistent differences in TFP levels across regions due to the presence of a time trend (Li & Papell, 1999b). Our findings loosely correspond with a few empirical studies on regional stochastic TFP convergence in the European regional scope. For example Byrne et al. (2009) show a lack of stochastic convergence of TFP for Italian regions. Similar conclusions are drawn by D'Uva and De Siano (2011). Interpreting these results, it should be noted that both mentioned studies are limited in the spatial scope, which makes it difficult to formulate a general conclusion.

In the next step, we analyze the $\beta$-convergence. Table 4.4 contains the estimation results of two models. The former allows us to verify the existence of the absolute $\beta$-convergence of TFP for the period 2008–2018. The latter considers a possible difference in convergence processes in two time-periods (2008–2013 and 2014–2018). For this purpose, the model includes a dummy regressor—*PP*, which takes the value 0 for 2008–2013 and 1 for 2014–2018, and its interaction with the autoregressive term—$TFP_{i,t-1}$.

**Table 4.4** Results from the absolute $\beta$-convergence model

| Dependent variable: $\text{TFP}_{i,t}$ | Model 1 | Model 2 |
|---|---|---|
| $\text{TFP}_{i,t-1}$ | 0.7742*** | 0.6887*** |
| | (0.0371) | (0.0421) |
| PP | $x$ | 0.0063 |
| | | (0.0064) |
| PP*$\text{TFP}_{i,t-1}$ | $x$ | −0.0320* |
| | | (0.0194) |
| Cons | 0.0663*** | 0.0913*** |
| | (0.0106) | (0.0116) |
| $\beta$ convergence test | 0.7742 | 0.6887 (2008–2013) |
| | (0.0000) | (0.0000) |
| | | 0.6556 (2014–2018) |
| | | (0.0000) |
| Convergence speed | 0.2559 | 0.3730 (2008–2013) |
| | | 0.4207 (2014–2018) |
| Autocorrelation test | −0.3344 | −0.2364 |
| | (0.7381) | (0.813) |
| N | 219 | 219 |

Notes: *, **, and *** indicate significance at the 1%, 5%, and 10% level. Robust standard errors are displayed in parentheses. $\beta$ convergence test displays $\beta$ parameter and $p$-value in Wald test, i.e. H0: $\beta = 1$, H1: $\beta < 1$. Autocorrelation test displays test statistic and $p$-value in Arellano-Bond test for zero second-order autocorrelation in first-differenced errors

The estimation of Model 1 indicates a positive and significant effect of the autoregressive term (0.7742), which confirms the absolute $\beta$-convergence hypothesis. The convergence speed is 0.2558. As regards Model 2, it shows that convergence process in the period 2014–2018 was more dynamic than in the period 2008–2013.

The revealed absolute $\beta$-convergence of TFP across European regions may result from the implementation of EU regional policy aimed at diminishing disparities among regions and member states, intended to pursue the goal of economic, social, and territorial cohesion. This is in line with findings of Celli et al. (2021), confirming that the EU regional policy played an important role in the economic recovery of the poorest regions in the aftermath of the Great Recession. However, the opposite results were demonstrated by Albanese et al. (2021) who did not find a positive effect of the European Regional Development Fund (ERDF) on local TFP growth in Southern Italy, the most backward regions of the country, between 2007 and 2015. Also Madeira et al. (2021) reveal that a poor Spanish region Extremadura, despite being eligible for EU funding as a convergence region by cohesion policy, diverged from the EU average between 2008 and 2014.

The obtained results indicating that convergence process across EU regions in 2014–2018 was more dynamic than in 2008–2013 may result from the fact that in the 2014–2020 programming period, EU regional policy changed significantly due to the implementation of the smart specialization strategies. Regional innovation policies, aiming at improving the capacity of regions to generate, transfer and acquire

**Table 4.5** Results from the $\beta$-convergence model with spatial effects

| Dependent variable: $\text{TFP}_{i,t}$ | Model 3 (W1) | Model 4 (W2) | Model 5 (W3) |
|---|---|---|---|
| $\text{TFP}_{i,t-1}$ | 1.3303*** | 1.3169*** | 1.8130*** |
| | (0.2045) | (0.2067) | (0.2469) |
| $w\text{TFP}_{i,t}$ | 1.2320*** | 1.1644*** | 0.0504*** |
| | (0.2811) | (0.2828) | (0.1224) |
| $w\text{TFP}_{i,t} * \text{TFP}_{i,t-1}$ | −3.3784*** | −3.2424*** | −0.1838*** |
| | (0.8290) | (0.8253) | (0.0368) |
| cons | −0.1513** | −0.1412** | −0.2056*** |
| | (0.0653) | (0.0666) | (0.0792) |
| $\beta$ convergence test | 0.4688 | 0.4878 | 0.4965 |
| | (0.0000) | (0.0000) | (0.0000) |
| Convergence speed | 0.7576 | 0.7178 | 0.7002 |
| Autocorrelation test | −0.8390 | −0.9373 | −0.8018 |
| | (0.4015) | (0.3486) | (0.4226) |
| $N$ | 219 | 219 | 219 |

Notes: *, **, and *** indicate significance at the 1%, 5%, and 10% level. Robust standard errors are displayed in parentheses. $\beta$ convergence test displays $\beta$ parameter at mean TFP in neighbouring regions and p-value in Wald test, i.e. H0: $\beta = 1$, H1: $\beta < 1$. Autocorrelation test displays test statistic and p-value in Arellano-Bond test for zero second-order autocorrelation in first-differenced errors

knowledge and innovation through implementation of smart specialization strategies, were assigned particular importance in the Innovation Union initiative of Europe 2020 strategy (Commission of the European Communities, 2010). As it was previously described, smart specialization strategies are place-based, focused on enhancing the capabilities and opportunities for technological development, taking into account the specific technological and human capital of the area. This profound shift in the directions of regional innovation policies enabled supporting the specific resources of regions increasing the effectiveness of public financing contributing to more dynamic development of lagging regions.

To address the issue of the spatial interdependencies of TFP regional convergence, we apply a spatial autoregressive model on panel data. The model uses three alternative spatial weights matrixes (i.e. W1—a first-order binary contiguity matrix, W2—a second-order binary contiguity matrix, W3—an inverse-distance matrix) to check the robustness of our results (Table 4.5). We introduce an interaction between the autoregressive term—$TFP_{i,t-1}$ and the spatially lagged TFP—$wTFP_{i,t}$. Hence, we allow the speed of convergence to vary according to the level of TFP in the neighbouring regions.

At the outset, it is worth noting that Model 3 provides results similar to those obtained in Model 4 and Model 5. As expected, TFP of the European regions are strongly affected by their spatial interdependence, which suggests that TFP convergence process has a spatial character. The spatially-lagged TFP coefficient indicates highly significant effects of TFP spillovers. Similar results are reported by Dettori et al. (2012). It should be noted that the coefficient associated with the autoregressive term drops sharply with the increase of TFP in neighbouring regions. For very low

**Table 4.6** Summary results for the log-$t$ test

| Club | No. of regions | $\widehat{b}$ | SE | $t$ | $\widehat{\alpha}$ | avTFP 2008 | avTFP 2018 |
|------|----------------|---------------|------|-------|--------------------|------------|------------|
| 1 | 56 | 0.1338 | 0.1832 | 0.7303 | 0.0669 | 0.1611 | 0.2013 |
| 2 | 112 | −0.0880 | 0.1667 | −0.5281 | −0.0440 | 0.2643 | 0.2978 |
| 3 | 51 | 0,3079 | 0.1821 | 1.6911 | 0.1540 | 0.2998 | 0.3579 |

Notes: $\widehat{\alpha}$—speed of convergence, applied truncation parameter—$r = 0.3$

levels of TFP in neighbouring regions, there is a tendency to TFP divergence. However, after reaching a threshold, TFP in neighbouring regions positively affects the speed of TFP convergence. A possible explanation is that positive externalities of TFP appear in groups of regions in which the external knowledge base is already quite developed and rich.

Our results correspond with the assumption made by Basile et al. (2011) that growth rate of a region depends not only on its initial conditions and on its own structural characteristics but also on initial conditions, structural characteristics and growth rates in neighbouring regions. This confirms the important role of spatial proximity in knowledge diffusion across regions and reinforces the effects generated by geographical closeness thanks to synergies and increasing returns.

Our findings indicate the existence of knowledge spillovers provided the determined level of productivity is achieved in regions. They are in line with evolutionary approach, assuming that the spatial processes of knowledge creation and distribution are cumulative, path-dependent, and interactive and that new knowledge is expected to be based on related, former sources of knowledge (Balland, 2016) and that the region's current resources impact its further capacity to produce knowledge (Heimeriks & Boschma, 2014). Due to the cumulative nature of knowledge, the convergence processes depend not only on the initial innovative potential of the regions and their capacity to absorb knowledge spillovers generated in other regions (Roper & Love, 2006; Verspagen, 2010).

To extend the $\beta$-convergence framework, we employ the log $t$ test proposed by Phillips and Sul (2007b). This approach allows us to identify local convergence clubs. The log $t$ test applied to the group of all panel units indicates that the null hypothesis of overall convergence is rejected at the 1% significance level ($-2.326$). It means that PS club clustering procedure may be used. Table 4.6 shows the final results for the club clustering and merging algorithms.

The $\widehat{b}$ value for Club 1 is significantly positive, but less than 2. It provides a strong evidence of conditional convergence, i.e. growth rates of TFP converge over time, but little evidence of level convergence within this club. The $\widehat{b}$ value for Club 1 is also positive, but not statistically different from zero. In turn, the $\widehat{b}$ value for Club 2 is negative, but not statistically different from zero. The lack of statistical significance of the $\widehat{b}$ values for Club 1 and Club 2 implies that these clubs are weaker convergence clubs than Club 3. The convergence speed $\widehat{\alpha}$ for Club 3 is 15%, whereas the values of $\widehat{\alpha}$ for Club 1 and Club 2 lack interpretations.

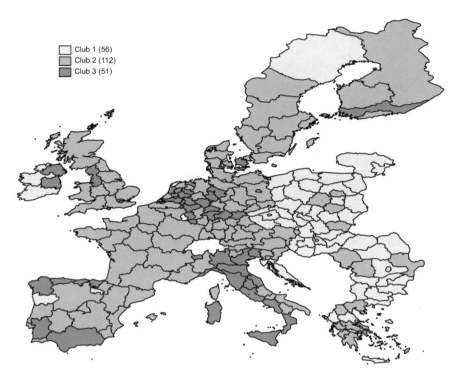

**Fig. 4.4** Spatial distribution of convergence club

The spatial distribution of clubs is presented in Fig. 4.4. Club 1 consists of the regions with the lowest level of TFP (0.1611 on average in 2008). The regions that converge in this club are located mostly in the Central-Eastern European countries (Poland—14 regions, Czech Republic—8 regions, Hungary—8 regions, Bulgaria—6 regions, Romania—5 regions) and Greece (5 regions). Club 2, with an average of TFP equal to 0.2643 in 2008, is spatially heterogeneous and contains about 50% of all regions. This club is dominated by the regions from Germany, France, and Spain. It also includes a large number of regions from the UK and the Netherlands. As regards Club 3 with the highest level of TFP (0.2998 on average in 2008), it is the least numerous and its core group is formed by the regions from Germany and Italy.

Figure 4.5 presents the relative transition paths for regions within a particular club. The transition path is determined by the transition coefficient $\widehat{h}_{it}$ (Eq. 4.20), which is calculated as the ratio of the individual region's log of TFP over time to the average of the log of TFP for panel units over time. As can be seen in graphs, the bundles of transition paths for all clubs take a form of a funnel. This tendency is most evident for Club 2 and Club 3. Furthermore, the transition seems to be uniform in the whole period.

Summing up, we find that both the stochastic technological convergence and the absolute $\beta$ type of technological convergence took place in the European regional

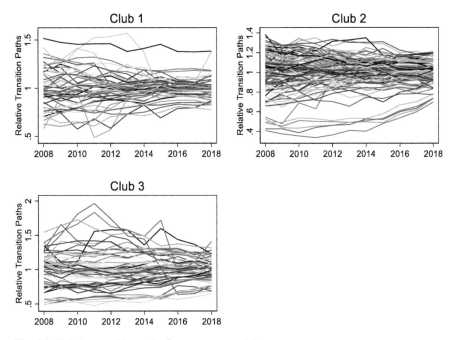

**Fig. 4.5** Relative transition paths for convergence clubs

space in the period 2008–2018. Moreover, the analysis of the $\beta$-convergence in the spatial context underscores the importance of technological interdependence among regions, which is reflected in the fact that a region's speed of convergence depends on the TFP levels of neighbouring regions.

Our results correspond with catching-up approach, as regions that are not capable to innovate and lag behind could benefit from the adoption of technological improvements developed by technologically leading regions. In consequence, they achieve a relatively faster rate of growth, ceteris paribus, that should lead to convergence process, provided they developed absorptive capacities (Alexiadis, 2012). We demonstrate that interregional connections and knowledge flows are shaped by spatial patterns and convergence is enhanced by spatial proximity. This is in line with the empirical results indicating that knowledge externalities across regional space have an impact on innovation performance (Bottazzi & Peri, 2003; Moreno et al., 2005; Roper et al., 2017). This finding supports the approach to technological externalities presented in the spatially augmented Solow models (Yu & Lee, 2012). The extension of our analysis to the multiple equilibria framework by applying the log $t$ test suggests the existence of conditional convergence in the clubs of regions. Interpreting this result it should be noted that regions which belong to different clubs in the short run may be slowly converging towards each other in the long run.

## 4.4  Impact of Innovation Activities on Processes of Regional Technological Convergence

To study the impact of innovation on TFP convergence in the European regions, two proxies for innovation activities are included as additional regressors in the Barro regression for panel data. This results in extending our research to the concept of conditional convergence, which assumes that each region possesses its own steady-state TFP growth rate that is conditional on innovation. As mentioned previously, comparable data on regional innovation are rather scarce. Similar to other previous works, we use R&D investments and patents as indicators of regional innovation (e.g. Acs et al., 2002; Baptista & Swann, 1998; Bode, 2004; Di Cagno et al., 2016; German-Soto & Flores, 2013; Jaffe, 1989). The former reflects regional innovation input and the latter relates to regional innovation output (Hauser et al., 2018). Although both indicators have several shortcomings (Acs et al., 2002; Guellec & van Pottelsberghe de la Potterie, 2001), they are still considered to be the most reliable single measures of cross-regional differences in innovation.

Table 4.7 contains the empirical results for the conditional $\beta$-convergence model. We include interactions between the autoregressive term—$TFP_{i,t-1}$ and innovation-related variables, i.e. $RD_{it}$ and $PAT_{it}$. In this way, we can observe how innovations affect the speed of convergence. The findings show that both R&D and patents

**Table 4.7** Results from the conditional $\beta$-convergence model

| Dependent variable: TFP$_{i,t}$ | Model 6 |
|---|---|
| TFP$_{i,t-1}$ | 1.1655*** |
|  | (0.0732) |
| RD$_{i,t}$ | 0.1146*** |
|  | (0.0251) |
| PAT$_{i,t}$ | 0.0257*** |
|  | (0.0084) |
| RD$_{i,t}$ * TFP$_{i,\,t-1}$ | −0.4130*** |
|  | (0.0894) |
| PAT$_{i,t}$ * TFP$_{i,t-1}$ | −0.0840*** |
|  | (0.0280) |
| Cons | −0.0296 |
|  | (0.0193) |
| $\beta$ convergence test | 0.5657 |
|  | (0.0000) |
| Convergence speed | 0.5697 |
| Autocorrelation test | −0.3377 |
|  | (0.7356) |
| $N$ | 219 |

Notes: *, **, and *** indicate significance at the 1%, 5%, and 10% level. Robust standard errors are displayed in parentheses. $\beta$ convergence test displays $\beta$ parameter at mean RD and PAT and $p$-value in Wald test, i.e. H0: $\beta = 1$, H1: $\beta < 1$. Autocorrelation test displays test statistic and $p$-value in Arellano-Bond test for zero second-order autocorrelation in first-differenced errors stimulate convergence processes after exceeding certain thresholds. One explanation for this fact is that there is a critical scale of innovation activities required to trigger convergence processes. Moreover, as the empirical evidence provided by Foray (2014) indicates there are substantial indivisibilities in knowledge production and the existence of economies of scale, economies of scope and spillovers is an essential determinant of the productivity of innovation activities. The positive impact of innovation on TFP convergence comes from decreasing effects of R&D investments and patenting activities. In other words, the higher the level of regional knowledge base, measured by TFP level, is, the less effective innovation activities are. Similarly, Burda and Severgnini (2018b), following the 'distance to the frontier' approach of Griffith et al. (2004), find that R&D investment acts as a source of TFP convergence, since for theGerman regions that are closer to the technological frontier additional R&D spending reduces TFP growth. These results are generally consistent with the conclusions of the semi-endogenous growth models of Jones (1995) and Kortum (1997b).

The results of estimation of the conditional $\beta$-convergence model with spatial effects are summarized in Table 4.8. By convention, the results are presented for the first-order contiguity matrix (Model 7), for the second-order contiguity matrix (Model 8), as well as for the inverse-distance matrix (Model 9). Our estimates indicate the relevance of knowledge externalities across regional economies in the process of TFP convergence. Interestingly, spatial spillovers due to R&D activity performed in other regions strongly affect the convergence process of a particular region. It is important that this finding is robust to the alternative weight matrices. The evidence corroborates the previous findings, which reveal the existence of R&D spillovers among the European regions. For example Abdelmoula and Legros (2009) prove that R&D spending of neighbouring regions affects positively a region's total factor productivity. With regard to patenting activity, the situation seems less obvious. For Model 8 with the second-order contiguity matrix, the increase of patenting activity of neighbouring regions impedes TFP convergence process of a particular region. In the case of two other models (Model 7 and Model 9) the interaction effect appears to be insignificant. One possible explanation for this finding is that the protection function of patent outweighs its information-sharing function, which facilitates knowledge spillovers by disclosing the specification of inventions. For example Song et al. (2022) report that patent lifetime affects the technological knowledge diffusion growth rate negatively. Another more plausible explanation is that a patent novelty requirement may hinder knowledge flows, since too much novelty of invention brings large cost of its absorption (Gilsing et al., 2008). As mentioned by Benoliel and Gishboliner (2022), novelty traps intensify in developing regions, where technology diffusion is costlier due to lower absorptive capacity.

In the next step, we consider initial conditions related to regional innovation systems (Table 4.1) that can explain the emergence of multiple steady-state equilibria across the European regions, which are identified by the log $t$ test. For this reason, we use the ordered logit model, where the variable to be explained represents the club to which a given region belongs. In Table 4.9 we report the results of the

**Table 4.8** Results from the conditional $\beta$-convergence model with spatial effects

| Dependent variable: $\text{TFP}_{i,t}$ | Model 7 | Model 8 | Model 9 |
|---|---|---|---|
| $\text{TFP}_{i,t-1}$ | 1.1755*** | 1.2517*** | 1.5331*** |
| | (0.0391) | (0.0431) | (0.0809) |
| $\text{RD}_{i,t}$ | 0.0449*** | 0.0273** | 0.0045** |
| | (0.0121) | (0.0123) | (0.0019) |
| $\text{PAT}_{i,t}$ | 0.0183*** | 0.0206*** | 0.0233** |
| | (0.0035) | (0.0035) | (0.0109) |
| $\text{wTFP}_{i,t}$ | 0.2184*** | 0.2114*** | 0.0156*** |
| | (0.0298) | (0.0323) | (0.0032) |
| $\text{wRD}_{i,t}$ | 0.1139*** | 0.1815*** | 0.0096*** |
| | (0.0167) | (0.0217) | (0.0014) |
| $\text{wPAT}_{i,t}$ | −0.0002 | −0.0141** | −0.0002 |
| | (0.0048) | (0.0058) | (0.0003) |
| $\text{RD}_{i,t} * \text{TFP}_{i,t-1}$ | −0.1983*** | −0.1357*** | −0.0998*** |
| | (0.039) | (0.0393) | (0.0357) |
| $\text{PAT}_{i,t} * \text{TFP}_{i,t-1}$ | −0.0547*** | −0.0607*** | −0.0412*** |
| | (0.0119) | (0.0118) | (0.0108) |
| $\text{wRD}_{i,t} * \text{TFP}_{i,t-1}$ | −0.3955*** | −0.646*** | −0.0354*** |
| | (0.0538) | (0.0701) | (0.0043) |
| $\text{wPAT}_{i,t} * \text{TFP}_{i,t-1}$ | −0.0051 | 0.0387** | −0.0006 |
| | (0.0159) | (0.0189) | (0.0009) |
| cons | −0.0796*** | −0.0939*** | −0.1301*** |
| | (0.0103) | (0.0114) | (0.0229) |
| $\beta$ convergence test | 0.4851 | 0.5028 | 0.4081 |
| | (0.0000) | (0.0000) | (0.0000) |
| Convergence speed | 0.7235 | 0.6875 | 0.8962 |
| $N$ | 219 | 219 | 219 |

Notes: *, **, and *** indicate significance at the 1%, 5%, and 10% level. Standard errors are displayed in parentheses. $\beta$ convergence test displays $\beta$ parameter at mean RD, PAT, wRD, wPAT in neighbour regions and $p$-value in Wald test, i.e. H0: $\beta = 1$, H1: $\beta < 1$

ordered logit model estimation and the marginal effects, calculated as a mean of marginal effects at each value of explanatory variables. These effects provide a direct and easily interpretable answer to the question of how changes in covariates affect the change in the probability of outcomes (club membership). To reduce the multicollinearity problem, we apply the backward stepwise approach, which leads to a reduced model that best explains the club formation process.

We can conclude that an increase in the number of innovative SMEs collaborating with others in the population of SMEs leads to convergence processes that take place in regions from Club 1. The inclusion of a given region in networks of collaboration and knowledge transfer structures significantly increases innovative potential as it allows to access to external knowledge that they are not able to create on their own (Mahroum, 2008; Matras-Bolibok et al., 2017). However, the benefits to a great extent depend on the abilities of individual institutions and areas, and are achieved by those that are best connected (in terms of the number and quality of networks to which they have access) and equipped with adequate human and

**Table 4.9** Results from the ordered logit model

| Dependent variable: club$_i$ | Model 10 Coef | Margins for Clubs | |
|---|---|---|---|
| COL$_i$ | −3.9341*** (1.2362) | 1 | 0.4968*** (0.1494) |
| | | 2 | 0.0347 (0.0457) |
| | | 3 | −0.5315*** (0.1640) |
| LLR$_i$ | 2.2150* (1.201501) | 1 | −0.2797* (0.1475) |
| | | 2 | −0.0195 (0.0334) |
| | | 3 | 0.2992*** (0.1636) |
| PPI$_i$ | 3.3726*** (0.0031) | 1 | −0.4259*** (0.1168) |
| | | 2 | −0.0297 (0.0477) |
| | | 3 | 0.4556*** (0.1337) |
| CIT$_i$ | 7.6961*** (1.3530) | 1 | −0.9719*** (0.1457) |
| | | 2 | −0.0678 (0.1053) |
| | | 3 | 1.0397*** (0.1687) |
| DES$_i$ | 0.0025*** (0.0105) | 1 | −0.00032* (0.00016) |
| | | 2 | −0.00002 (0.00003) |
| | | 3 | 0.00034* (0.00018) |
| cut1 | 2.6166 (0.4999) | | |
| cut2 | 5.9357 (0.6525) | | |
| Pseudo R$^2$ | 0.2329 | | |
| LR chi$^2$ | 95.80 (0.0000) | | |
| N | 200 | | |

Notes: *, **, and *** indicate significance at the 1%, 5%, and 10% level. Standard errors are displayed in parentheses

technical resources necessary to absorb and use knowledge obtained from outside effectively. Regions with weaker innovation potential are forced to bear not only the higher costs of instant access to network structures but also of reducing the innovation gap to the leaders. Thus, cooperation in innovation activities in regions with a low innovation potential may be difficult and ineffective initially and bring results only in the long run, provided the improvement of their innovation capabilities.

On the other hand, a rise in human capital measured as the share of the population aged 25–64 enrolled in education or training aimed at improving knowledge, skills, and competences, stimulates convergence processes peculiar to regions with the highest TFP level (Club 3). As expected, in line with the empirical evidence and theoretical considerations, human capital is a crucial factor that determines the productivity and innovation performance of a given economy (Diebolt & Hippe, 2022), as there are several channels through which human capital may affect technological progress (Acemoglu & Autor, 2012). According to Nelson and Phelps (1966b), human capital not only determines the ability to create innovation, but also contributes to diminishing the technological gap between more and less developed economies through imitation and absorption of innovation. Most importantly, the same conclusions as for human capital can be drawn on the impact of product and process innovations on convergence processes in regions with the highest TFP level. In line with our expectations, implementation of innovation contributes to a better TFP performance (Mohnen & Hall, 2013). It is worth to indicate that the impact of innovation performance on productivity level depends on the type of innovation, however the evidence is ambiguous. This could result from the fact that product and process innovations often appear together and their individual contribution is hard to assess (Jaumandreu & Mairesse, 2017). For example empirical evidence presented by Hall (2011) indicates that product innovations have an economic impact on productivity, while the impact of process innovations is more ambiguous. Peters et al. (2017) report that in German high-tech industries product innovation increases productivity, whereas in low-tech industries—process innovation. Moreover, as Demmel et al. (2017) demonstrate, the level of development is also a mediating factor in the innovation–productivity link.

As regards intellectual property rights in the form of designs, they also generate convergence processes peculiar to regions from Club 3. This is in line with previous evidence in the literature indicating that intellectual property rights have a great impact on productivity and innovativeness (Chang et al., 2018; Habib et al., 2019). As Su et al. (2022) demonstrate, the linkage of IPR protection to TFP is negative in least-developed countries that offer the weakest protection and inverted U-shaped in developing and developed countries with the strongest IPR protection. Moreover, the optimal IPR protection level for TFP is greater in developed than in developing countries. What is worth to point out, as Chen et al. (2013) reveal, patent-oriented R&D productivity growth serves as the main source of national R&D productivity growth than the journal article-oriented one. However, we finally find that the increase in the share of the most cited scientific publications in the total number of scientific publications has the positive influence on the probability of belonging to Club 3. Publications are considered as a strong proxy for the real amount of science-driven (Pasteur-type) research, given the requirement to publish the results of scientific R&D. The higher quality of publications, on average, is, the greater impact on innovation performance in terms of citations in subsequent publications (Varga et al., 2014). It is worth to point out that knowledge production processes are becoming ever more interregional as a growing number of cross-regional collaboration in scientific publications is observed (Barrios et al., 2019b). Scientific collaboration makes the knowledge production more efficient and shortens the time for obtaining research results due to division of labour (Coccia & Bozeman, 2016). Moreover it leads to an increase in scientific productivity and a higher impact of publications (Bozeman et al., 2013).

In the last step of our analysis, we endogenously determine clubs of regions on the basis of a full set of conditioning variables associated with regional innovation systems (Table 4.1). Following RIS (European Commission, 2021) methodology and applying the TOPSIS method we identify four regional innovation clubs: Emerging Innovators, Moderate Innovators, Strong Innovators, and Innovation Leaders. The most innovative regions, on average, lead in most of the indicators. They score particularly well in the field of patent applications and public-private co-publications. The best performance of Strong Innovators is observed in the fields of trademark and individual design applications and lifelong learning. Moderate Innovators obtain the highest results in the level of sales of new-to-market and new-to-enterprise product innovations as a percentage of total turnover. The group of the least innovative regions outperforms the innovation performance of the other groups in the level of non-R&D innovation expenditures. The relatively high performance of Emerging Innovators in this field may mean that in less innovative regions enterprises innovate by purchasing external knowledge embedded mainly in advanced machinery and equipment.

Figure 4.6 presents the spatial distribution of the regional innovation club members. As can be seen, the group of the most innovative regions in EU, belonging to the Innovation Leaders club, is the most numerous and consists of 54 regions that are located along the UK–Germany–Switzerland corridor and in Scandinavian countries—Finland and Sweden. The lowest levels of innovation performance are present in peripheral regions of Eastern and South-Eastern Europe, mainly in Romania, Bulgaria, Poland, and Greece. It can be observed, that the innovation performance distribution across European regions is interrelated with TFP distribution.

Table 4.10 shows the results of the absolute $\beta$-convergence model for individual regional innovation clubs.

Basing on the data presented in Table 4.10, the main conclusion that can be derived is that innovations accelerate TFP convergence. More precisely, the group of Emerging Innovators converges very slowly with TFP levels. This group is also characterized by the lowest average level of TFP in the whole period. The convergence speed and the average level of TFP rise gradually moving across the two middle groups to the group of Innovation Leaders, which experiences the highest speed of TFP convergence and the highest average level of TFP over the analyzed period. It is worth noting that the results received from both our approaches to club convergence testing prove to be qualitatively similar.

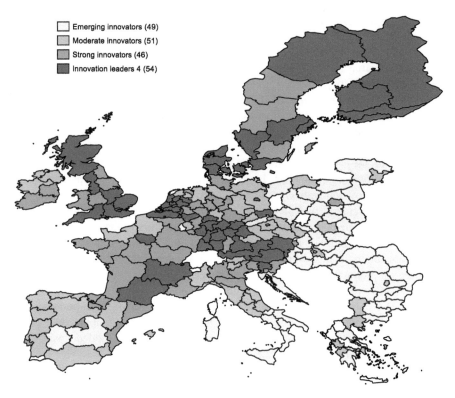

**Fig. 4.6** Regional innovation clubs

**Table 4.10** Results from the absolute $\beta$-convergence model for regional innovation clubs

| Dependent variable: TFP$_{i,t}$ | Model 11 (Emerging innovators) | Model 12 (Moderate innovators) | Model 13 (Strong innovators) | Model 14 (Innovation leaders) |
|---|---|---|---|---|
| TFP$_{i\ t-1}$ | 0.9414*** (0.0203) | 0.8553*** (0.0257) | 0.7164*** (0.0802) | 0.6040*** (0.0506) |
| Cons | 0.0165*** (0.0038) | 0.0434*** (0.0086) | 0.0934*** (0.0259) | 0.1326*** (0.0163) |
| $\beta$ convergence test | 0.9414 (0.0019) | 0.8553 (0.0000) | 0.7164 (0.0002) | 0.6040 (0.0000) |
| Convergence speed | 0.0604 | 0.1563 | 0.3335 | 0.5041 |
| Autocorrelation test | −0.3513 (0.7254) | 0.5262 (0.5988) | −0.7355 (0.4620) | 2.2123 (0.0269) |
| N | 49 | 51 | 46 | 54 |

Notes: *, **, and *** indicate significance at the 1%, 5%, and 10% level. Robust standard errors are displayed in parentheses. $\beta$ convergence test displays $\beta$ parameter and $p$-value in Wald test, i.e. H0: $\beta = 1$, H1: $\beta < 1$. Autocorrelation test displays test statistic and $p$-value in Arellano-Bond test for zero second-order autocorrelation in first-differenced errors

# References

Abdelmoula, M., & Legros, D. (2009). Interregional R D spillovers in Europe. *Region et Developpement, 30*, 101–118.

Acemoglu, D., & Autor, D. (2012). What does human capital do? A review of Goldin and Katz's he race between education and technology. *Journal of Economic Literature, 50*(2), 426–463. https://doi.org/10.1257/jel.50.2.426

Acs, Z., Anselin, L., & Varga, A. (2002). Patents and innovation counts as measures of regional production of new knowledge. *Research Policy, 31*(7), 1069–1085.

Albanese, G., de Blasio, G., & Locatelli, A. (2021). Does EU regional policy promote local TFP growth? Evidence from the Italian Mezzogiorno. *Papers in Regional Science, 100*(2), 327–348. https://doi.org/10.1111/pirs.12574

Alexiadis, S. (2012). *Convergence clubs and spatial externalities: Models and applications of regional convergence in Europe.* Springer.

Arthur, W. B. (1989). Competing technologies, increasing returns, and lock-in by historical events. *The Economic Journal, 99*(394), 116–131. https://doi.org/10.2307/2234208

Balland, P.-A. (2016). Relatedness and the geography of innovation. In *Handbook on the geographies of innovation* (pp. 127–141). Edward Elgar. Accessed from https://econpapers.repec.org/bookchap/elgeechap/16055_5f6.htm

Baptista, R., & Swann, P. (1998). Do firms in clusters innovate more? *Research Policy, 27*(5), 525–540. https://doi.org/10.1016/S0048-7333(98)00065-1

Barrios, C., Flores, E., Martínez, M. Á., & Ruiz-Martínez, M. (2019b). Is there convergence in international research collaboration? An exploration at the country level in the basic and applied science fields. *Scientometrics, 120*(2), 631–659. https://doi.org/10.1007/s11192-019-03133-9

Basile, R., Capello, R., & Caragliu, A. (2011). Interregional knowledge spillovers and economic growth: The role of relational proximity. Advances in spatial Science. In K. Kourtit, P. Nijkamp, & R. Stough (Eds.), *Drivers of innovation, entrepreneurship and regional dynamics* (pp. 21–43). Springer. Accessed from https://ideas.repec.org/h/spr/adspcp/978-3-642-17940-2_2.html

Benoliel, D., & Gishboliner, M. (2022). Daniel Benoliel & Michael Gishboliner, Novelty Traps, Kiwis, and other flight-less birds. *Michigan State Law Review, 2020*, 5.

Beugelsdijk, S., Klasing, M. J., & Milionis, P. (2018). Regional economic development in Europe: The role of total factor productivity. *Regional Studies, 52*(4), 461–476. https://doi.org/10.1080/00343404.2017.1334118

Blundell, R., & Bond, S. (1998). Initial conditions and moment restrictions in dynamic panel data models. *Journal of Econometrics, 87*(1), 115–143. https://doi.org/10.1016/S0304-4076(98)00009-8

Bode, E. (2004). The spatial pattern of localized R&D spillovers: An empirical investigation for Germany. *Journal of Economic Geography, 4*(1), 43–64.

Bottazzi, L., & Peri, G. (2003). Innovation and spillovers in regions: Evidence from European patent data. *European Economic Review, 47*(4), 687–710.

Bouayad-Agha-Hamouche, S., & Védrine, L. (2010). Estimation strategies for a spatial dynamic panel using GMM. A new approach to the convergence issue of European regions. *Spatial Economic Analysis, 5*(2), 205–227.

Bozeman, B., Fay, D., & Slade, C. P. (2013). Research collaboration in universities and academic entrepreneurship: The-state-of-the-art. *The Journal of Technology Transfer, 38*(1), 1–67. https://doi.org/10.1007/s10961-012-9281-8

Breitung, J., & Pesaran, M. H. (2008). Unit roots and Cointegration in panels. In L. Mátyás & P. Sevestre (Eds.), *The econometrics of panel data* (Vol. 46, pp. 279–322). Springer. https://doi.org/10.1007/978-3-540-75892-1_9

Burda, M. C., & Severgnini, B. (2018b). Total factor productivity convergence in German states since reunification: Evidence and explanations. *Journal of Comparative Economics, 46*(1), 192–211.

Byrne, J., Fazio, G., & Piacentino, D. (2009). Total factor productivity convergence among Italian regions: Some evidence from panel unit root tests. *Regional Studies, 43*(1), 63–76.

Capello, R., & Lenzi, C. (2013). *Territorial patterns of innovation: An inquiry on the knowledge economy in European regions.* Routledge.

Capello, R., & Lenzi, C. (2015). Knowledge, innovation and productivity gains across European regions. *Regional Studies, 49*(11), 1788–1804. https://doi.org/10.1080/00343404.2014.917167

Celli, V., Cerqua, A., & Pellegrini, G. (2021). Does R&D expenditure boost economic growth in lagging regions? *Social Indicators Research.* https://doi.org/10.1007/s11205-021-02786-5

Chang, X., McLean, R. D., Zhang, B., & Zhang, W. (2018). *Do patents portend productivity growth? Global evidence from private and public firms (SSRN Scholarly Paper No. 2371600).* https://doi.org/10.2139/ssrn.2371600

Chen, C.-P., Hu, J.-L., & Yang, C.-H. (2013). Produce patents or journal articles? A cross-country comparison of R&D productivity change. *Scientometrics, 94*(3), 833–849.

Coccia, M., & Bozeman, B. (2016). Allometric models to measure and analyze the evolution of international research collaboration. *Scientometrics, 108*(3), 1065–1084. https://doi.org/10.1007/s11192-016-2027-x

Commission of the European Communities. (2010). *Europe 2020. A strategy for smart, suitable and inclusive growth.* COM (2010)2020. European Commission.

D'Uva, M., & De Siano, R. (2011). Time series approaches to Italian regional convergence. *Applied Economics, 43*(29), 4549–4559.

Demmel, M. C., Mañez, J. A., Rochina-Barrachina, M. E., & Sanchis-Llopis, J. A. (2017). Product and process innovation and total factor productivity: Evidence for manufacturing in four Latin American countries. *Review of Development Economics, 21*(4), 1341–1363.

Dettori, B., Marrocu, E., & Paci, R. (2012). Total factor productivity, intangible assets and spatial dependence in the European regions. *Regional Studies, 46*(10), 1401–1416. https://doi.org/10.1080/00343404.2010.529288

Di Cagno, D., Fabrizi, A., Meliciani, V., & Wanzenböck, I. (2016). The impact of relational spillovers from joint research projects on knowledge creation across European regions. *Technological Forecasting and Social Change, 108*(C), 83–94.

Diebolt, C., & Hippe, R. (2022). The long-run impact of human capital on innovation and economic growth in the regions of Europe. In *Frontiers in economic history* (pp. 85–115). Springer. Accessed from https://ideas.repec.org/h/spr/frochp/978-3-030-90858-4_5.html

European Commission. (2021). *Regional Innovation Scoreboard 2021.* Methodology report. European Commission.

Foray, D. (2014). From smart specialisation to smart specialisation policy. *European Journal of Innovation Management, 17*(4), 492–507. https://doi.org/10.1108/EJIM-09-2014-0096

Fratesi, U., & Senn, L. (2009). Regional growth, connections and economic modelling: An introduction. In U. Fratesi & L. Senn (Eds.), *Growth and innovation of competitive regions: The role of internal and external connections* (pp. 3–27). Springer. https://doi.org/10.1007/978-3-540-70924-4_1

Frees, E. W. (1995). Assessing cross-sectional correlation in panel data. *Journal of Econometrics, 69*(2), 393–414.

Frees, E. W. (2004). *Longitudinal and panel data: Analysis and applications in the social sciences.* Cambridge University Press.

German-Soto, V., & Flores, L. G. (2013). Assessing some determinants of the regional patenting: An essay from the Mexican states. *Technology and Investment, 4*(3), 1–9. https://doi.org/10.4236/ti.2013.43B001

Gilsing, V., Nooteboom, B., Vanhaverbeke, W., Duysters, G., & van den Oord, A. (2008). Network embeddedness and the exploration of novel technologies: Technological distance, betweenness centrality and density. *Research Policy, 37*(10), 1717–1731. https://doi.org/10.1016/j.respol.2008.08.010

Griffith, R., Redding, S., & Van Reenen, J. (2004). Mapping the two faces of R&D: Productivity growth in a panel of OECD industries. *Review of Economics and Statistics, 86*(4), 883–895. https://doi.org/10.1162/0034653043125194

Guellec, D., & van Pottelsberghe de la Potterie, B. (2001). The internationalisation of technology analysed with patent data. *Research Policy, 30*(8), 1253–1266.

Habib, M., Abbas, J., & Noman, R. (2019). Are human capital, intellectual property rights, and research and development expenditures really important for total factor productivity? An empirical analysis. *International Journal of Social Economics, 46*(6), 756–774.

Hall, B. H. (2011). *Innovation and productivity (SSRN Scholarly Paper No. 1879040)*. Accessed from https://papers.ssrn.com/abstract=1879040

Hauser, C., Siller, M., Schatzer, T., Walde, J., & Tappeiner, G. (2018). Measuring regional innovation: A critical inspection of the ability of single indicators to shape technological change. *Technological Forecasting and Social Change, 129*(C), 43–55.

Heimeriks, G., & Boschma, R. (2014). The path- and place-dependent nature of scientific knowledge production in biotech 1986–2008. *Journal of Economic Geography, 14*(2), 339–364.

Hernández-Salmerón, M. H., & Romero-Ávila, D. (2015). Convergence in output and its sources among industrialised countries. In *SpringerBriefs in economics*. Springer. Accessed from https://ideas.repec.org/b/spr/spbrec/978-3-319-13635-6.html

Hospers, G.-J. (2003). Beyond the Blue Banana? *Intereconomics, 38*(2), 76–85. https://doi.org/10.1007/BF03031774

Hwang, C. L., & Yoon, K. (1981). *Multiple attribute decision making: Methods and applications: A state-of-the-art survey*. Springer.

Islam, N. (1995b). Growth empirics: A panel data approach. *The Quarterly Journal of Economics, 110*(4), 1127–1170. https://doi.org/10.2307/2946651

Jaffe, A. (1989). Real effects of academic research. *American Economic Review, 79*(5), 957–970.

Jaumandreu, J., & Mairesse, J. (2017). Disentangling the effects of process and product innovation on cost and demand. *Economics of Innovation and New Technology, 26*(1–2), 150–167. https://doi.org/10.1080/10438599.2016.1205276

Jones, C. (1995). R&D-based models of economic growth. *Journal of Political Economy, 103*(4), 759–784.

Kortum, S. S. (1997b). Research, patenting, and technological change. *Econometrica, 65*(6), 1389–1419. https://doi.org/10.2307/2171741

Li, Q., & Papell, D. (1999b). Convergence of international output time series evidence for 16 OECD countries. *International Review of Economics & Finance, 8*(3), 267–280.

Madeira, P. M., Vale, M., & Mora-Aliseda, J. (2021). Smart specialisation strategies and regional convergence: Spanish Extremadura after a period of divergence. *Economies, 9*(4), 138. https://doi.org/10.3390/economies9040138

Mahroum, S., & National Endowment for Science, Technology and the Arts (Great Britain). (Eds.). (2008). *Innovation by adoption: Measuring and mapping absorptive capacity in UK nations and regions*. NESTA.

Marrocu, E., Paci, R., & Usai, S. (2013). Productivity growth in the old and new Europe: The role of agglomeration externalities. *Journal of Regional Science, 53*(3), 418–442.

Matras-Bolibok, A., Bolibok, P., & Kijek, T. (2017). *Effectiveness of collaboration on innovation activity in EU regions*.

McKelvey, R. D., & Zavoina, W. (1975). A statistical model for the analysis of ordinal level dependent variables. *The Journal of Mathematical Sociology, 4*(1), 103–120. https://doi.org/10.1080/0022250X.1975.9989847

Mohnen, P., & Hall, B. H. (2013). Innovation and productivity: An update. *Eurasian Business Review, 3*(1), 47–65. https://doi.org/10.14208/BF03353817

Moreno, R., Paci, R., & Usai, S. (2005). Spatial spillovers and innovation activity in European regions. *Environment and Planning A: Economy and Space, 37*(10), 1793–1812. https://doi.org/10.1068/a37341

Moscone, F., & Tosetti, E. (2009). A review and comparison of tests of cross-section independence in panels. *Journal of Economic Surveys, 23*(3), 528–561. https://doi.org/10.1111/j.1467-6419. 2008.00571.x

Nelson, R. R., & Phelps, E. S. (1966b). Investment in humans, technological diffusion, and economic growth. *The American Economic Review, 56*(1/2), 69–75. https://doi.org/10.1016/ B978-0-12-554002-5.50015-7

Neuländtner, M., & Scherngell, T. (2022). R&D networks and their effects on knowledge exploration versus knowledge exploitation: Evidence from a spatial econometric perspective. *Industry and Innovation, 1–32*, 847. https://doi.org/10.1080/13662716.2022.2063110

Ng, S., & Perron, P. (1995). Unit root tests in ARMA models with data-dependent methods for the selection of the truncation lag. *Journal of the American Statistical Association, 90*(429), 268–281. https://doi.org/10.1080/01621459.1995.10476510

O'Donnell, C. J. (2011b). DPIN version 1.0: A program for decomposing productivity index numbers. In *CEPA working papers series*. University of Queensland. Accessed from https:// ideas.repec.org/p/qld/uqcepa/69.html

Ord, J. K., & Getis, A. (1995). Local spatial autocorrelation statistics: Distributional issues and an application. *Geographical Analysis, 27*(4), 286–306. https://doi.org/10.1111/j.1538-4632.1995. tb00912.x

Pesaran, M. H. (2004). *General diagnostic tests for cross section dependence in panels*. University of Cambridge, Faculty of Economics, Cambridge Working Papers in Economics No. 0435. https://doi.org/10.17863/CAM.5113

Pesaran, M. H. (2007). A simple panel unit root test in the presence of cross-section dependence. *Journal of Applied Econometrics, 22*(2), 265–312.

Peters, B., Roberts, M. J., Vuong, V. A., & Fryges, H. (2017). Estimating dynamic R&D choice: An analysis of costs and long-run benefits. *The Rand Journal of Economics, 48*(2), 409–437. https:// doi.org/10.1111/1756-2171.12181

Phillips, P. C. B., & Sul, D. (2007b). Transition modeling and econometric convergence tests. *Econometrica, 75*(6), 1771–1855.

Phillips, P. C. B., & Sul, D. (2009b). Economic transition and growth. *Journal of Applied Econometrics, 24*(7), 1153–1185. https://doi.org/10.1002/jae.1080

Puškárová, P., & Piribauer, P. (2016). The impact of knowledge spillovers on total factor productivity revisited: New evidence from selected European capital regions. *Economic Systems, 40*(3), 335–344.

Roper, S., & Love, J. (2006). Innovation and regional absorptive capacity: The labour market dimension. *The Annals of Regional Science, 40*(2), 437–447.

Roper, S., Love, J. H., & Bonner, K. (2017). Firms' knowledge search and local knowledge externalities in innovation performance. *Research Policy, 46*(1), 43–56. https://doi.org/10. 1016/j.respol.2016.10.004

Schatzer, T., Siller, M., Walde, J., & Tappeiner, G. (2019b). The impact of model choice on estimates of regional TFP. *International Regional Science Review, 42*(1), 98–116. https://doi. org/10.1177/0160017618754311

Song, H., Hou, J., & Zhang, Y. (2022). Patent protection: Does it promote or inhibit the patented technological knowledge diffusion? *Scientometrics, 127*(5), 2351–2379.

Su, Z., Wang, C., & Peng, M. W. (2022). Intellectual property rights protection and total factor productivity. *International Business Review, 31*(3), 101956. https://doi.org/10.1016/j.ibusrev.2021.101956

Varga, A., Pontikakis, D., & Chorafakis, G. (2014). Metropolitan Edison and cosmopolitan Pasteur? Agglomeration and interregional research network effects on European R&D productivity. *Journal of Economic Geography, 14*(2), 229–263. https://doi.org/10.1093/jeg/lbs041

Verspagen, B. (2010). The spatial hierarchy of technological change and economic development in Europe. *The Annals of Regional Science, 45*(1), 109–132. https://doi.org/10.1007/s00168-009-0293-8

Yu, J., & Lee, L.-F. (2012). Convergence: A spatial dynamic panel data approach. *Global Journal of Economics (GJE), 01*(01), 1–36.

# Chapter 5
# Conclusions

This book tries to make new contributions to the current research on the link between innovation and technological convergence in the European regions. From the theoretical perspective, an attempt is made to provide a detailed view of the issue of catching-up and speeding-up effects of innovation activities in the technology race of regions by considering various conceptual approaches rooted in R&D-based endogenous growth theory, technology gap theory and innovation geography. As far as the methodological aspect of the research is concerned, the multi-faceted approach to testing TFP convergence in the sample of 219 European regions in the period 2008–2018 is applied.

Consistent with prior research, we reveal a high degree of dispersion in TFP distribution across European regions. We demonstrate that the most productive regions in EU are placed along the UK–Germany–Italy corridor, whereas the lowest levels of TFP are present in peripheral regions of Eastern and South-Eastern Europe. We also observe significant interregional dispersion in regional TFP within countries and conclude that it might arise from different efficiency of the innovation and regional policy pursued at the national level in order to reduce interregional disparities. Moreover, the results indicate the existence of east-west and north-south divisions in TFP clustering.

We find that both the stochastic technological convergence and the absolute β-type technological convergence took place in European regional space in the period 2008–2018. We conclude that the revealed absolute β-convergence of TFP across European regions may result from the implementation of EU regional policy, intended to pursue the goal of economic, social, and territorial cohesion. Our results indicate that convergence process across EU regions in 2014–2018 was more dynamic than in 2008–2013. It may arise from the significant change in the directions of regional innovation policies in the 2014–2020 programming period due to the implementation of the smart specialization strategies which enabled the increase in the effectiveness of public financing and contributed to more dynamic development of less developed regions.

© The Author(s) 2023
T. Kijek et al., *Innovation and Regional Technological Convergence*, SpringerBriefs in Regional Science, https://doi.org/10.1007/978-3-031-24531-2_5

Moreover, the results of the analysis of the β-convergence in the spatial context reveal the existence of technological interdependence between regions evinced by the dependence of the convergence speed of a given region on TFP levels of contiguous regions. This confirms the significant role of spatial proximity in innovation diffusion across regions due to occurrence of synergy effects and increasing returns. Our results correspond with the catching-up approach as technologically lagged regions that are not capable to innovate could benefit from the adoption of technological improvements developed by innovation leaders.

Applying conditional β-convergence model, we present the impact of innovation on the speed of convergence. Our results show that both R&D investments and patenting activities stimulate convergence processes. The results of estimation of the conditional β-convergence model with spatial effects indicate the importance of knowledge externalities across regional economies in the process of TFP convergence. We reveal that spatial spillovers due to R&D activity performed in other regions impact have a strong impact on the convergence process of a given region. However, regarding the impact of patenting activity on the speed of convergence our results remain inconclusive.

Extending the β-convergence framework, we identify three local clubs differing in patterns of convergence in TFP. We demonstrate that initial conditions related to regional innovation systems can explain the emergence of multiple steady-state equilibria across European regions. We conclude that an increase of innovative SMEs collaborating with others leads to convergence processes that take place in the club of regions with the lowest TFP level. On the other hand, human capital, product and process innovation, intellectual property rights in the form of designs, and the share of the most cited scientific publications stimulate convergence processes peculiar to regions with the highest TFP level.

Basing on variables reflecting the performance of regional innovation systems, we endogenously determine four innovation clubs of regions: Emerging Innovators, Moderate Innovators, Strong Innovators, and Innovation Leaders. The results of the absolute β-convergence model for individual regional innovation clubs indicate that innovations accelerate TFP convergence. We conclude that the convergence speed and the average level of TFP rise gradually with the level of regional innovativeness. We demonstrate that the regional club characterized with the lowest levels of innovation performance (Emerging Innovators) and lowest average level of TFP converges very slowly with TFP levels, whereas the club of Innovation Leaders achieves the highest speed of TFP convergence and the highest average level of TFP over the analyzed period.

Evaluation of the role of innovation in the processes of technological convergence in the European regional area is crucial from the standpoint of the effectiveness of regional and innovation policy. The revealed existence of TFP convergence clubs requires a sustainable model of policy actions focused on promoting both the advantages of the strongest regions and the development opportunities in the lagging ones. Our results demonstrating that the convergence speed and the average level of TFP rise gradually with the level of regional innovativeness provide empirical support for the formulation and implementation of innovation policies which would be more tuned to the initial and structural characteristics of particular regions.

Printed by Printforce, the Netherlands